Simply
vegetarian

Simply

vegetarian

100 fuss-free recipes for everyday cooking

Bath • New York • Cologne • Melbourne • Delhi
Hong Kong • Shenzhen • Singapore

This edition published by Parragon Books Ltd in 2016

Parragon Books Ltd
Chartist House
15–17 Trim Street
Bath BA1 1HA, UK
www.parragon.com

Introduction by Linda Doeser
Cover photography by Clive Streeter
Additional photography by Clive Bozzard-Hill
Additional food styling by Val Barrett

ISBN: 978-1-4748-5056-8

Printed in China

Notes for the Reader
This book uses both metric and imperial measurements. Follow
the same units of measurement throughout; do not mix metric and
imperial. All spoon measurements are level: teaspoons are assumed
to be 5 ml, and tablespoons are assumed to be 15 ml. Unless otherwise stated, milk is assumed to be full fat, eggs and individual fruits
and vegetables are medium, pepper is freshly ground black pepper
and salt is table salt. Unless otherwise stated, all root vegetables
should be peeled prior to using.

The times given are an approximate guide only. Preparation times
differ according to the techniques used by different people and the
cooking times may also vary from those given.

Recipes using raw or very lightly cooked eggs should be avoided
by infants, the elderly, pregnant women, convalescents and anyone
suffering from an illness. Pregnant and breastfeeding women are
advised to avoid eating peanuts and peanut products. Sufferers
from nut allergies should be aware that some of the ready-made
ingredients used in the recipes in this book may contain nuts.
Always check the packaging before use.

Vegetarians should be aware that some of the ready-made
ingredients used in the recipes in this book may contain animal
products. Always check the packaging before use.

Contents

Introduction

In the last two or three decades, increasing numbers of people have turned to a vegetarian diet. As a result, recipes for vegetarian dishes, once heavily dependent on beans, pasta and cheese, have become wonderfully varied and innovative. This period has also coincided with exponential growth in international travel that has provided the opportunity for people to explore the cuisines of many other cultures, including those with a long-standing vegetarian tradition, such as the Indian sub-continent and South-east Asia. The popular holiday destinations of southern Europe and the Mediterranean have also offered inspiration as, although their cuisines are by no means vegetarian, they feature a vast array of superb vegetable dishes.

In fact, vegetarian dishes have become so mainstream that they play a major role on the menus of upmarket restaurants in towns and cities throughout the country. Even non-vegetarians relish such delicious treats as warm goat's cheese salad and caramelized onion tart, not because they are vegetarian or are thought to be healthy, but because they look so appetizing and taste so delectable.

Like any diet, a vegetarian one can be good or bad. It may surprise some people to learn that vegetarian dishes are not automatically healthy, although it is certainly true that the Western diet tends to include unhealthy amounts of meat, animal products and saturated fats. It is equally true that a diet that contains a high proportion of vegetables, including beans and other pulses, is good for the heart and digestive system, helps protect against a number of diseases and is rich in vitamins and many minerals. It is easier for meat-eaters to obtain enough protein, as animal products contain all the essential amino acids, the building blocks of proteins. Virtually no vegetarian ingredient contains all these essential amino acids, but many contain some of them – nuts, pulses, grains, tofu, eggs, cheese and other dairy products. Combining these different ingredients ensures that a meal contains what is known as complete protein. This often happens automatically, so, for example, a vegetarian chilli containing kidney beans will usually be served on a bed of rice and this combination of beans and grain contains all the essential amino acids.

However, rather than worrying about whether there is a balance of nuts or dairy products, the best way to ensure that a vegetarian diet is healthy is to make it as varied as possible.

Top Tips for Success

• Always check the labels on products when shopping to avoid inadvertently buying animal products. Standard Worcestershire sauce, for example, contains anchovies, but a vegetarian version is available. Some block margarines contain fish oils, while some low-fat spreads include gelatine. Labels will also identify brands fortified with vitamins, such as B12 and D, and this can be important for vegans and vegetarians who eat few dairy products. Some soft cheeses, such as ricotta, cream cheese and curd cheese, don't usually contain rennet, an animal enzyme used in the production of harder cheeses, but check the label before buying.

• Buy vegetables and fruit in peak condition, preferably locally grown and seasonal, as lengthy transportation depletes the vitamin content. Store vegetables in a cool, dark place and don't leave them standing or soaking in water for a long time after preparing them.

• Buy spices in small quantities and store them in a cool, dark place as they quickly lose their aroma and flavour. For the best flavour, buy whole spices and grind them yourself.

• Buy nuts and seeds in small quantities as, if they are left too long, they will become rancid because of their high oil content.

• Store pulses in an airtight container in a cool, dark place. Make a note of the 'use by' or 'best before' date as, after about six months, the skins become tough and they require much longer cooking. When using canned pulses, drain and rinse them to remove any sugar and/or salt used in processing.

• Store tofu in the refrigerator. Once opened, it will keep for up to a week in a bowl of cold water in the refrigerator; change the water daily.

• Iron is a particularly important mineral for teenage girls and young women but the human body is less efficient at absorbing it from vegetable than from animal sources. When serving iron-rich foods – dark green leafy vegetables, tofu and pulses – include something rich in vitamin C at the same meal as this increases the uptake. Avoid drinking tea at the meal as tannin decreases the uptake.

• Too much fat, especially saturated fat, is not good in any diet, vegetarian or otherwise. Eggs, cheese, cream and some other dairy products have a high fat content and should be used sparingly. Look for low-fat or reduced fat alternatives. Semi-skimmed and skimmed milk have the same nutritional value as full-fat.

1

Super Soups & Starters

creamy tomato & basil soup

SERVES 6

25 g/1 oz butter

1 tbsp olive oil

1 onion, finely chopped

1 garlic clove, chopped

900 g/2 lb plum tomatoes, chopped

700 ml/1¼ pints vegetable stock

125 ml/4 fl oz dry white wine

2 tbsp sun-dried tomato purée

2 tbsp torn fresh basil leaves, plus extra leaves to garnish

150 ml/5 fl oz double cream

salt and pepper

1 Melt the butter with the oil in a large, heavy-based saucepan. Add the onion and cook, stirring occasionally, for 5 minutes, or until softened. Add the garlic, tomatoes, stock, wine and tomato purée, stir well and season to taste. Partially cover the saucepan and simmer, stirring occasionally, for 20–25 minutes, or until the mixture is soft and pulpy.

2 Remove the saucepan from the heat, leave to cool slightly, then pour into a blender or food processor. Add the torn basil and process. Push the mixture through a sieve into a clean saucepan with a wooden spoon.

3 Stir in the cream and reheat the soup, but do not let it boil. Ladle the soup into warmed bowls, garnish with the basil leaves and serve immediately.

mixed bean soup

SERVES 4

1 onion, chopped

**1 garlic clove,
finely chopped**

2 celery sticks, sliced

1 large carrot, diced

**400 g/14 oz canned
chopped tomatoes**

150 ml/5 fl oz dry red wine

**1.2 litres/2 pints vegetable
stock**

1 tsp dried oregano

**425 g/15 oz canned mixed
beans and pulses,
drained**

2 courgettes, diced

1 tbsp tomato purée

salt and pepper

**shop-bought pesto,
to garnish**

1 Place the prepared onion, garlic, celery and carrot in a large saucepan. Stir in the tomatoes, red wine, vegetable stock and oregano.

2 Bring the vegetable mixture to the boil, cover and leave to simmer for 15 minutes. Stir the mixed beans and pulses into the mixture with the courgettes, and continue to cook, uncovered, for a further 5 minutes.

3 Add the tomato purée to the mixture and season well with salt and pepper to taste. Then heat through, stirring occasionally, for a further 2–3 minutes, but be careful not to allow the mixture to boil again.

4 Ladle the soup into warmed bowls and serve immediately with a spoonful of pesto on each portion.

watercress soup

SERVES 4

**2 bunches of watercress
(about 200 g/7 oz),
thoroughly cleaned**

40 g/1½ oz butter

2 onions, chopped

**225 g/8 oz potatoes,
roughly chopped**

**1.2 litres/2 pints vegetable
stock or water**

**whole nutmeg,
for grating (optional)**

salt and pepper

**125 ml/4 fl oz crème
fraîche, to serve**

1 Remove the leaves from the stalks of the watercress and set aside. Roughly chop the stalks. Melt the butter in a large saucepan over a medium heat, add the onions and cook for 4–5 minutes, until soft. Do not brown.

2 Add the potatoes and mix well with the onions. Add the watercress stalks and the stock.

3 Bring to the boil, then reduce the heat, cover and simmer for 15–20 minutes, until the potato is soft.

4 Add the watercress leaves and stir in to heat through. Remove from the heat and transfer to a blender or food processor. Process until smooth and return the soup to the rinsed-out saucepan. Reheat and season to taste with salt and pepper. Add a good grating of nutmeg, if using.

5 Ladle into warmed bowls with the crème fraîche spooned on top and an extra grating of nutmeg, if desired. Serve immediately.

vegetable & corn chowder

SERVES 4

1 tbsp vegetable oil

1 red onion, diced

1 red pepper, deseeded and diced

3 garlic cloves, crushed

300 g/10½ oz potatoes, diced

2 tbsp plain flour

600 ml/1 pint milk

300 ml/10 fl oz vegetable stock

50 g/2 oz broccoli florets

300 g/10½ oz canned sweetcorn, drained

75 g/2¾ oz Cheddar cheese, grated

salt and pepper

1 Heat the oil in a large saucepan. Add the onion, red pepper, garlic and potatoes and sauté over a low heat, stirring frequently, for 2–3 minutes.

2 Stir in the flour and cook, stirring, for 30 seconds. Gradually stir in the milk and stock.

3 Add the broccoli and sweetcorn. Bring the mixture to the boil, stirring constantly, then reduce the heat and simmer for about 20 minutes, or until all the vegetables are tender.

4 Stir in 50 g/1¾ oz of the cheese until it melts. Season to taste and ladle into warmed bowls. Garnish with the remaining cheese and serve immediately.

borscht

SERVES 6

1 onion

55 g/2 oz butter

350 g/12 oz raw beetroot, cut into thin batons, and 1 raw beetroot, grated

1 carrot, cut into thin batons

3 celery sticks, thinly sliced

2 tomatoes, peeled, deseeded and chopped

1.4 litres/2½ pints vegetable stock

1 tbsp white wine vinegar

1 tbsp sugar

2 large fresh dill sprigs

115 g/4 oz white cabbage, shredded

salt and pepper

150 ml/5 fl oz soured cream, to garnish

1 Slice the onion into rings. Melt the butter in a large, heavy-based saucepan. Add the onion and cook over a low heat, stirring occasionally, for 3–5 minutes, or until softened. Add the beetroot batons, carrot, celery and chopped tomatoes and cook, stirring frequently, for 4–5 minutes.

2 Add the stock, vinegar, and sugar and snip a tablespoon of dill into the saucepan. Season to taste with salt and pepper. Bring to the boil, reduce the heat and simmer for 35–40 minutes, or until the vegetables are tender.

3 Stir in the cabbage, cover and simmer for 10 minutes. Stir in the grated beetroot, with any juices, and cook for a further 10 minutes. Ladle into warmed bowls. Garnish with a spoonful of soured cream and another tablespoon of snipped dill and serve immediately.

carrot & cumin soup

SERVES 4–6

3 tbsp butter or margarine

1 large onion, chopped

1–2 garlic cloves, crushed

350 g/12 oz carrots, sliced

900 ml/1½ pints vegetable stock

¾ tsp ground cumin

2 celery sticks, thinly sliced

115 g/4 oz potato, diced

2 tsp tomato purée

2 tsp lemon juice

2 bay leaves

about 300 ml/10 fl oz skimmed milk

salt and pepper

celery leaves, to garnish

1 Melt the butter or margarine in a large pan. Add the onion and garlic and cook very gently until softened.

2 Add the carrots and cook gently for a further 5 minutes, stirring frequently and taking care they do not brown.

3 Add the stock, cumin, seasoning, celery, potato, tomato purée, lemon juice and bay leaves and bring to the boil. Cover and simmer for about 30 minutes until the vegetables are tender.

4 Remove and discard the bay leaves, cool the soup a little and then press it through a sieve or process in a food processor or blender until smooth.

5 Pour the soup into a clean pan, add the milk and bring to the boil over a low heat. Taste and adjust the seasoning if necessary. Ladle the soup into warmed bowls, garnish each serving with a small celery leaf and serve immediately.

pepper & chilli soup

SERVES 4

225 g/8 oz red peppers, seeded and sliced

1 onion, sliced

2 garlic cloves, crushed

1 green chilli, chopped

300 ml/10 fl oz passata

600 ml/1 pint vegetable stock

2 tbsp chopped basil, plus extra leaves to garnish

salt and pepper

1 Put the sliced red peppers in a large saucepan with the onion, garlic and chilli. Add the passata and the vegetable stock and bring to the boil, stirring well.

2 Reduce the heat to a simmer and continue to cook the vegetables for 20 minutes, or until the peppers have softened. Drain, reserving the liquid and vegetables separately.

3 Using the back of a spoon, press the vegetables through a sieve. Alternatively, process in a food processor until smooth.

4 Return the vegetable purée to a clean saucepan with the reserved cooking liquid. Add the basil, season and heat through until hot. Ladle the soup into warmed bowls, garnish with the basil and serve immediately.

white bean soup

SERVES 4

**175 g/6 oz dried cannellini
beans, soaked in cold
water to cover overnight**

**1.5 litres/2¾ pints vegetable
stock**

**115 g/4 oz dried corallini,
conchigliette piccole,
or other soup pasta**

6 tbsp olive oil

2 garlic cloves, finely chopped

**4 tbsp chopped fresh
flat-leaf parsley**

salt and pepper

**fresh crusty bread,
to serve**

1 Drain the soaked beans and place them in a large, heavy-based saucepan. Add the stock and bring to the boil. Partially cover the pan, then reduce the heat and simmer for 2 hours, or until tender.

2 Transfer about half the beans and a little of the stock to a food processor or blender and process to a smooth purée. Return the purée to the pan and stir well to mix. Return to the boil.

3 Add the pasta, return to the boil and cook for 10 minutes, or until tender.

4 Meanwhile, heat 4 tablespoons of the olive oil in a small saucepan. Add the garlic and cook over a low heat, stirring frequently, for 4–5 minutes, or until golden. Stir the garlic mixture into the soup and add the parsley. Season with salt and pepper and ladle into warmed soup bowls. Drizzle with the remaining olive oil and serve immediately with crusty bread.

lettuce & rocket soup

SERVES 4–6

1 tbsp butter

1 large onion, halved and sliced

2 leeks, sliced

1.5 litres/2¾ pints vegetable stock

85 g/3 oz white rice

2 carrots, thinly sliced

3 garlic cloves

1 bay leaf

2 heads soft round lettuce (about 450 g/1 lb), cored and chopped

175 ml/6 fl oz double cream

freshly grated nutmeg

85 g/3 oz rocket leaves, finely chopped, plus extra leaves to garnish

salt and pepper

1 Melt the butter in a large saucepan over a medium heat and add the onion and leeks. Cover and cook for 3–4 minutes, stirring frequently, until the vegetables begin to soften.

2 Add the stock, rice, carrots, garlic and bay leaf with a large pinch of salt. Bring just to the boil. Reduce the heat, cover and simmer for 25–30 minutes, or until the rice and vegetables are tender. Remove the bay leaf.

3 Add the lettuce to the saucepan and cook for 10 minutes, until the leaves are soft, stirring occasionally.

4 Allow the soup to cool slightly, then transfer to a blender or a food processor and purée until smooth, working in batches if necessary. (If using a food processor, strain off the cooking liquid and reserve. Purée the soup solids with enough cooking liquid to moisten them, then combine with the remaining liquid.)

5 Return the soup to the saucepan and place over a low-medium heat. Stir in the cream, reserving a little for the garnish, and the nutmeg. Simmer for 5 minutes, stirring occasionally, until the soup is reheated.

6 Add the rocket leaves and simmer for 2–3 minutes, stirring occasionally, until wilted. Adjust the seasoning and ladle the soup into warmed bowls. Garnish each serving with a swirl of cream and a rocket leaf, and serve immediately.

creamed mushrooms

SERVES 4

juice of 1 small lemon

450 g/1 lb small button mushrooms

25 g/1 oz butter

1 tbsp sunflower or olive oil

1 small onion, finely chopped

125 ml/4 fl oz whipping or double cream

1 tbsp chopped fresh parsley, plus 4 sprigs, to garnish

salt and pepper

1 Sprinkle a little of the lemon juice over the mushrooms. Heat the butter and oil in a frying pan, add the onion and cook for 1 minute. Add the mushrooms, shaking the pan so they do not stick.

2 Season to taste with salt and pepper, then stir in the cream, chopped parsley and remaining lemon juice.

3 Heat until hot but do not allow to boil, then transfer to individual bowls and garnish with the parsley sprigs. Serve immediately.

hot garlic-stuffed mushrooms

SERVES 4

4 large field mushrooms

4 sprays olive oil

2–3 garlic cloves, crushed

2 shallots

25 g/1 oz fresh wholemeal breadcrumbs

few fresh basil sprigs, plus extra to garnish

25 g/1 oz ready-to-eat dried apricots, chopped

1 tbsp pine kernels

55 g/2 oz feta cheese

pepper

1 Preheat the oven to 180°C/350°F/Gas Mark 4. Remove the stalks from the mushrooms and set aside. Spray the bases of the mushrooms with the oil and place underside up in a roasting tin.

2 Put the mushroom stalks in a food processor with the garlic, shallots and breadcrumbs. Reserve a few basil sprigs for the garnish then place the remainder in the food processor with the apricots, pine kernels and feta cheese. Add pepper to taste.

3 Process for 1–2 minutes, or until a stuffing consistency is formed, then divide among the mushroom caps.

4 Bake for 10–12 minutes, or until the mushrooms are tender and the stuffing is crisp on the top. Serve garnished with basil sprigs.

mini roast vegetable skewers

SERVES 4

1 red pepper, deseeded

1 yellow pepper, deseeded

1 large courgette

1 aubergine

2 tbsp olive oil

3 garlic cloves, crushed

salt and pepper

dip

2 tbsp chopped fresh dill

2 tbsp chopped fresh mint

250 ml/9 fl oz natural yoghurt

1 Preheat the oven to 200°C/400°F/Gas Mark 6. Cut the vegetables into 2 cm/¾ inch chunks. Place in a roasting tin large enough to hold them in a single layer.

2 Mix the olive oil and garlic together and drizzle over the top. Season well with salt and pepper then toss together. Roast for 25–30 minutes until tender and lightly charred.

3 Meanwhile, stir the dill and mint into the yoghurt. Spoon into four serving bowls.

4 When the vegetables are cool enough to handle, divide them between 12 cocktail sticks. Serve warm or cold with the bowls of dip on the side.

vegetable tartlets

MAKES 12

butter, for greasing

12 ready-baked puff pastry cases

2 tbsp olive oil

1 red pepper, deseeded and diced

1 garlic clove, crushed

1 small onion, finely chopped

225 g/8 oz ripe tomatoes, chopped

1 tbsp torn fresh basil

1 tsp fresh or dried thyme

salt and pepper

green salad, to serve

1 Preheat the oven to 200°C/400°F/Gas Mark 6 and grease several baking trays.

2 Place the ready-baked pastry cases on the prepared baking trays.

3 Heat the oil in a frying pan, add the pepper, garlic and onion and cook over a high heat for about 3 minutes until soft.

4 Add the tomatoes, herbs and seasoning and spoon onto the pastry cases.

5 Bake for about 5 minutes, or until the filling is piping hot. Serve warm with a green salad.

hummus

SERVES 8

225 g/8 oz dried chickpeas, covered with water and soaked overnight

juice of 2 large lemons

150 ml/5 fl oz tahini paste

2 garlic cloves, crushed

4 tbsp extra virgin olive oil

small pinch of ground cumin

1 tsp paprika

1 tbsp chopped fresh flat-leaf parsley

salt and pepper

pitta bread, to serve

1 Drain the chickpeas, put in a saucepan and cover with cold water. Bring to the boil, then simmer for about 2 hours, until very tender.

2 Drain the chickpeas, reserving a little of the liquid, and put in a food processor, reserving a few to garnish. Blend the chickpeas until smooth, gradually adding the lemon juice and enough of the reserved liquid to form a smooth, thick purée. Add the tahini paste, garlic, 3 tablespoons of the oil and the cumin and blend until smooth. Season to taste with salt and pepper.

3 Turn the mixture into a shallow serving dish and chill in the refrigerator for 2–3 hours before serving. To serve, mix the remaining oil with the paprika and drizzle over the top of the dish. Sprinkle with parsley and the reserved chickpeas. Serve immediately, with warm pitta bread.

mushroom pâté

SERVES 4

15 g/½ oz dried porcini mushrooms

1 tsp olive oil

2 shallots, finely chopped

2 garlic cloves, crushed

1 fresh jalapeño chilli, deseeded and finely chopped

2 celery sticks, trimmed and finely chopped

225 g/8 oz closed cup mushrooms, wiped and sliced

grated rind and juice of 1 orange

25 g/1 oz fresh breadcrumbs

1 tbsp chopped fresh parsley

1 small egg, beaten

pepper

raw vegetable sticks and crisp breads, to serve

1 Preheat the oven to 180°C/350°F/Gas Mark 4. Put the dried mushrooms in a bowl and cover with almost boiling water. Leave to soak for 30 minutes then drain, chop and reserve.

2 Heat the oil in a medium heavy-based saucepan, then add the shallots, garlic, chilli and celery. Cook, stirring frequently for 3 minutes, then add both the dried and fresh mushrooms and cook for a further 2 minutes.

3 Add the orange juice and continue to cook for 3–4 minutes, or until the mushrooms have collapsed. Remove the pan from the heat and stir in the orange rind, breadcrumbs, parsley, beaten egg and pepper to taste. Mix well.

4 Spoon the mixture into 4 individual ramekin dishes and level the surfaces. Place the dishes in a small baking tin and pour enough water to come halfway up the sides of the ramekins.

5 Bake for 15–20 minutes, or until a skewer inserted in the centre of each ramekin comes out clean. Remove and either leave to stand for 10 minutes before serving warm or chill until ready to serve. Turn out and serve with vegetable sticks and crisp breads.

aubergine pâté

SERVES 4–6

2 large aubergines

4 tbsp extra virgin olive oil

**2 garlic cloves,
very finely chopped**

4 tbsp lemon juice

salt and pepper

**2 tbsp roughly chopped
fresh flat-leaf parsley,
to garnish**

6 crisp breads, to serve

1 Preheat the oven to 180°C/350°F/Gas Mark 4. Score the skins of the aubergines with the point of a sharp knife, without piercing the flesh, and place them on a baking sheet. Bake for 1¼ hours, or until soft.

2 Remove the aubergines from the oven and leave until cool enough to handle. Cut them in half and, using a spoon, scoop out the flesh into a bowl. Mash the flesh thoroughly.

3 Gradually beat in the olive oil then stir in the garlic and lemon juice. Season to taste with salt and pepper. Cover with clingfilm and store in the refrigerator until required. Sprinkle with the parsley and serve with crisp breads.

stuffed aubergine slices

SERVES 4

1 medium aubergine

4 tbsp extra virgin olive oil

115 g/4 oz mozzarella cheese, grated

1 tbsp fresh chopped basil

400 g/14 oz canned tomatoes with added herbs, heated through

extra basil leaves, to garnish

1 Preheat the oven to 200°C/400°F/Gas Mark 6. Slice the aubergine lengthways into 8 slices. Brush the slices with oil and place on an ovenproof tray. Bake for 10 minutes, without letting them get too floppy. Remove from the oven. Scatter the grated cheese and basil over the aubergine slices.

2 Roll up each slice and place the slices in a single layer in a shallow ovenproof dish. Pour over the chopped tomatoes and cook in the oven for 10 minutes or until the sauce bubbles and the cheese melts.

3 Remove the stuffed aubergine slices from the oven and transfer carefully to serving plates. Spoon any remaining chopped tomatoes on or around the aubergine slices. Garnish with basil leaves and serve while still hot.

quesadillas

SERVES 4

**4 tbsp finely chopped fresh
jalapeño chillies**

1 onion, chopped

1 tbsp red wine vinegar

5 tbsp extra virgin olive oil

**300–400 g/10½–14 oz
canned sweetcorn**

8 soft flour tortillas

1 Put the chillies, onion, vinegar and 4 tablespoons of olive oil in a food processor or blender and process until finely chopped. Tip into a bowl and stir in the sweetcorn.

2 Heat the remaining oil in a frying pan, add a tortilla and cook for 1 minute until golden.

3 Spread a quarter of the chilli mixture over the tortilla and fold over.

4 Cook for 2–3 minutes until golden and the filling is heated through. Remove from the pan and keep warm. Repeat with the other tortillas and filling. Serve immediately.

spring rolls

MAKES 12

2 spring onions, plus a few more to garnish

5 dried Chinese mushrooms or fresh open-cap mushrooms

1 large carrot

55 g/2 oz canned bamboo shoots

55 g/2 oz Chinese leaves

2 tbsp vegetable oil, plus extra for deep-frying

225 g/8 oz beansprouts

1 tbsp soy sauce

12 spring roll wrappers

1 egg, beaten

salt

1 To make the garnish, make several cuts into the stem of each spring onion and place in a bowl of iced water until the tassels open out.

2 Place the mushrooms in a small bowl and cover with warm water. Leave to soak for 20–25 minutes, then drain and squeeze out the excess water. Remove the tough centres and slice the mushroom caps thinly. Cut the carrot and bamboo shoots into very thin julienne strips. Chop the 2 spring onions and shred the Chinese leaves.

3 Heat 2 tablespoons of oil in a preheated wok. Add the mushrooms, carrot and bamboo shoots and stir-fry for 2 minutes. Add the spring onions, Chinese leaves, beansprouts and soy sauce. Season to taste with salt and stir-fry for 2 minutes. Cool.

4 Divide the mixture into 12 equal portions and place one portion on the edge of each spring roll wrapper. Fold in the sides and roll up each one, brushing the join with beaten egg to seal. Heat the oil for deep-frying in a large, heavy-based saucepan to 180–190°C/350–375°F, or until a cube of bread browns in 30 seconds. Add the spring rolls, in batches, and cook for 4–5 minutes, or until golden and crispy. Take care that the oil is not too hot or the rolls will brown on the outside before cooking on the inside. Drain on kitchen paper. Keep warm. Garnish with spring onion tassels and serve.

roasted vegetable & feta cheese wraps

MAKES 4

1 red onion,
cut into eighths

1 red pepper, cored and
cut into eighths

1 small aubergine,
cut into eighths

1 courgette,
cut into eighths

4 tbsp extra virgin olive oil

1 clove of garlic, crushed

100 g/3½ oz feta cheese,
crumbled

small bunch of fresh mint,
shredded

4 x 25-cm/10-inch
sun-dried tomato wraps

salt and pepper

1 Preheat the oven to 220°C/425°F/Gas Mark 7. Mix all of the vegetables, olive oil, garlic and salt and pepper together and place in the oven in a non-stick oven tray. Roast for 15–20 minutes or until golden and cooked through.

2 Remove from the oven and leave to cool. Once cool, mix in the feta and mint.

3 Preheat a non-stick pan or grill pan until almost smoking, then cook the wraps one at a time on both sides for 10 seconds. This will add some colour and also soften the wraps.

4 Divide the vegetable and feta mixture between the wraps, placing it along the middle of each wrap. Roll up the wraps, cut them in half and serve.

filo-wrapped asparagus

SERVES 4

dip

85 g/3 oz natural cottage cheese

1 tbsp semi-skimmed milk

4 spring onions, trimmed and finely chopped

2 tbsp chopped fresh mixed herbs, such as basil, mint and tarragon

pepper

asparagus

20 asparagus spears

5 sheets filo pastry

lemon wedges, to serve

1 Preheat the oven to 190°C/375°F/Gas Mark 5. To make the dip, put the cottage cheese in a bowl and add the milk. Beat until smooth then stir in the spring onions, chopped herbs and pepper to taste. Place in a serving bowl, cover lightly and chill in the refrigerator until required.

2 Cut off and discard the woody end of the asparagus and shave with a vegetable peeler to remove any woody parts from the spears.

3 Cut the filo pastry into quarters and place one sheet on a work surface. Brush lightly with water then place a spear at one end. Roll up to encase the spear, and place on a large baking sheet. Repeat until all the asparagus spears are wrapped in pastry.

4 Bake for 10–12 minutes, or until the pastry is golden. Serve the spears with lemon wedges and the dip on the side.

pepper & basil pots

SERVES 4

1 tsp olive oil

2 shallots, finely chopped

2 garlic cloves, crushed

2 red peppers, peeled, deseeded and sliced into strips

1 orange pepper, peeled, deseeded and sliced into strips

4 tomatoes, thinly sliced

2 tbsp shredded fresh basil

pepper

salad leaves, to serve

1 Lightly brush 4 ramekin dishes with the oil. Mix the shallots and garlic together in a bowl and season with pepper to taste.

2 Layer the red and orange peppers with the tomatoes in the prepared ramekin dishes, sprinkling each layer with the shallot mixture and shredded basil. When all the ingredients have been added, cover lightly with clingfilm or baking paper. Weigh down using small weights and leave in the refrigerator for at least 6 hours, or preferably overnight.

3 When ready to serve, remove the weights and carefully run a knife around the edges. Invert onto serving plates and serve with salad leaves.

tomato bruschetta

SERVES 4

8 slices of rustic bread

4 garlic cloves, halved

8 plum tomatoes, peeled and diced

extra virgin olive oil, for drizzling

salt and pepper

fresh basil leaves, to garnish

1 Preheat the grill. Lightly toast the bread on both sides. Rub each piece of toast with half a garlic clove and then return to the grill for a few seconds.

2 Divide the diced tomatoes among the toasts. Season to taste with salt and pepper and drizzle with olive oil. Serve immediately, garnished with basil leaves.

wild mushroom bruschetta

SERVES 4

4 slices sourdough bread, such as Pugliese

3 garlic cloves, 1 halved and 2 crushed

2 tbsp extra virgin olive oil

225 g/8 oz mixed wild mushrooms, such as ceps, chanterelles and field mushrooms

1 tbsp olive oil

25 g/1 oz butter

1 small onion or 2 shallots, finely chopped

50 ml/2 fl oz dry white wine or Marsala

salt and pepper

2 tbsp roughly chopped fresh flat-leaf parsley, to garnish

1 Preheat the grill. Lightly toast the bread on both sides. Rub with the garlic halves and drizzle with the extra virgin olive oil. Transfer to a baking sheet and keep warm.

2 Wipe the mushrooms thoroughly to remove any trace of soil and slice any large ones. Heat the olive oil with half the butter in a frying pan, add the mushrooms and cook over a medium heat, stirring frequently, for 3–4 minutes until soft. Remove with a slotted spoon and keep warm.

3 Heat the remaining butter in the frying pan, add the onion and crushed garlic and cook over a medium heat, stirring frequently, for 3–4 minutes until soft. Add the wine, stir well and leave to bubble for 2–3 minutes until reduced and thickened. Return the mushrooms to the frying pan and heat through. The sauce should be thick enough to glaze the mushrooms. Season to taste with salt and pepper.

4 Pile the mushrooms on top of the warm bruschetta, scatter with the parsley and serve immediately.

VARIATION

For a slightly different flavour, add chopped tomatoes to the mushrooms. Then grate some cheese on top of the warm mushrooms and tomatoes.

2

Light Bites

warm goat's cheese salad

SERVES 4

1 small iceberg lettuce, torn into pieces

handful of rocket leaves

few radicchio leaves, torn

6 slices French bread

115 g/4 oz goat's cheese, sliced

dressing

4 tbsp extra virgin olive oil

1 tbsp white wine vinegar

salt and pepper

1 Preheat the grill. Divide all the leaves between 4 individual salad bowls.

2 Toast one side of the bread under the grill until golden. Place a slice of cheese on top of each untoasted side and toast until the cheese is just melting.

3 Put all the dressing ingredients into a bowl and beat together until combined. Pour over the leaves, tossing to coat.

4 Cut each slice of bread in half and place 3 halves on top of each salad. Toss very gently to combine and serve warm.

tomato & feta salad

SERVES 4

1 kg/2 lb 4 oz ripe tomatoes, thickly sliced

225 g/8 oz feta cheese

125 ml/4 fl oz extra virgin olive oil

16 black olives, stoned

pepper

1 Arrange the tomato slices in concentric rings on a serving dish. Crumble the feta over the tomatoes and drizzle with the olive oil. Top with the olives.

2 Season to taste with pepper. Salt is probably not necessary because feta is already quite salty. Leave to stand for 30 minutes before serving.

moroccan tomato & red pepper salad

SERVES 4

3 red peppers

4 ripe tomatoes

½ bunch of fresh coriander, chopped

2 garlic cloves, finely chopped

salt and pepper

1 Preheat the grill. Place the peppers on a baking sheet and cook under the grill, turning occasionally, for 15 minutes. Add the tomatoes and grill, turning occasionally, for a further 5–10 minutes, or until all the skins are charred and blistered. Remove from the heat and leave to cool.

2 Peel and deseed the peppers and tomatoes and slice the flesh thinly. Place in a bowl, mix well and season with salt and pepper. Sprinkle with the coriander and garlic, cover with clingfilm and chill in the refrigerator for at least 1 hour. Just before serving, drain off any excess liquid.

crunchy thai-style salad

SERVES 4

1 slightly under ripe mango

5 Romaine or Cos lettuce leaves, torn into pieces

100 g/3½ oz beansprouts

handful of fresh coriander leaves

25 g/1 oz roasted unsalted peanuts, crushed

dressing

juice of 1 lime

2 tbsp light soy sauce

1 tsp soft light brown sugar

1 shallot, very thinly sliced

1 garlic clove, finely chopped

1 red bird's eye chilli, very thinly sliced

1 tbsp chopped fresh mint

1 To make the dressing, mix the lime juice, soy sauce and sugar together in a bowl then stir in the shallot, garlic, chilli and mint.

2 Peel the mango using a sharp knife or potato peeler. Slice the flesh from either side and around the stone. Thinly slice or shred the flesh.

3 Place the torn lettuce, beansprouts, coriander leaves and mango in a serving bowl. Gently toss together. Spoon the dressing over the top, scatter with the peanuts and serve immediately.

red onion, tomato & herb salad

SERVES 4

900 g/2 lb tomatoes, sliced thinly

1 tbsp sugar (optional)

1 red onion, sliced thinly

large handful coarsely chopped fresh herbs

salt and pepper

dressing

2–4 tbsp vegetable oil

2 tbsp red wine vinegar or fruit vinegar

1 Arrange the tomato slices in a shallow bowl. Sprinkle with sugar (if using) and salt and pepper.

2 Separate the onion slices into rings and scatter over the tomatoes. Sprinkle the herbs over the top. Anything that is in season can be used – for example, tarragon, sorrel, coriander or basil.

3 Put the dressing ingredients in a jar with a screw-top lid. Shake well. Pour the dressing over the salad and mix gently.

4 Cover with clingfilm and refrigerate for 20 minutes. Remove the salad from the refrigerator 5 minutes before serving, unwrap the dish and stir gently before serving.

wilted spinach, yogurt & walnut salad

SERVES 2

450 g/1 lb fresh spinach leaves

1 onion, chopped

1 tbsp olive oil

225 ml/8 fl oz natural yogurt

1 garlic clove, finely chopped

2 tbsp chopped toasted walnuts

2–3 tsp chopped fresh mint

salt and pepper

pitta bread, to serve

1 Put the spinach and onion into a saucepan, cover and cook gently for a few minutes until the spinach has wilted.

2 Add the oil and cook for a further 5 minutes. Season to taste with salt and pepper. Combine the yogurt and garlic in a bowl.

3 Put the spinach and onion into a serving bowl and pour over the yogurt mixture. Scatter over the walnuts and chopped mint and serve with pitta bread.

french bean & walnut salad

SERVES 2

450 g/1 lb French beans

1 small onion, finely chopped

1 garlic clove, chopped

4 tbsp freshly grated Parmesan-style vegetarian cheese

2 tbsp chopped walnuts or almonds, to garnish

dressing

3 tbsp extra virgin olive oil

2 tbsp white wine vinegar

2 tsp chopped fresh tarragon

salt and pepper

1 Top and tail the beans, but leave them whole. Cook for 3–4 minutes in salted boiling water. Drain well, run under the cold tap to refresh and drain again. Put into a mixing bowl and add the onion, garlic and cheese.

2 Put all the dressing ingredients in a jar with a screw-top lid. Shake well. Pour the dressing over the salad and toss gently to coat. Cover with clingfilm and chill for at least 30 minutes.

3 Remove the beans from the refrigerator 10 minutes before serving. Give them a quick stir and transfer to an attractive, shallow serving dish.

4 Toast the nuts in a dry frying pan over a medium heat for 2 minutes, or until they begin to brown. Sprinkle the toasted nuts over the beans to garnish before serving.

avocado salad with lime dressing

SERVES 4

60 g/2¼ oz mixed red and green lettuce leaves

60 g/2¼ oz wild rocket

4 spring onions, finely diced

5 tomatoes, sliced

25 g/1 oz walnuts, toasted and chopped

2 avocados

1 tbsp lemon juice

lime dressing

1 tbsp lime juice

1 tsp French mustard

1 tbsp sour cream

1 tbsp chopped fresh parsley or coriander

3 tbsp extra-virgin olive oil

pinch of sugar

salt and pepper

1 Wash and drain the lettuce and rocket, if necessary. Shred all the leaves and arrange in the bottom of a large salad bowl. Add the spring onions, tomatoes and walnuts.

2 Stone, peel and thinly slice or dice the avocados. Brush with the lemon juice to prevent discoloration, then transfer to the salad bowl. Gently mix together.

3 To make the dressing, put all the dressing ingredients in a screw-top jar and shake well. Drizzle over the salad and serve immediately.

nutty beetroot salad

SERVES 4

3 tbsp red wine vinegar or fruit vinegar

3 cooked beetroot, grated

2 tart apples, eg Granny Smith

2 tbsp lemon juice

4 tbsp pecans

4 large handfuls mixed salad leaves

dressing

50 ml/2 fl oz plain yoghurt

50 ml/2 fl oz mayonnaise

1 garlic clove, chopped

1 tbsp chopped fresh dill

salt and pepper

1 Sprinkle vinegar over the beetroot, cover with clingfilm and chill for at least 4 hours.

2 Core and slice the apples, place the slices in a dish and sprinkle with the lemon juice.

3 Put all the dressing ingredients in a small bowl. Remove the beetroot from the refrigerator and dress. Add the apples to the beetroot and mix gently to coat with the salad dressing.

4 Toast the pecans in a dry frying pan over a medium heat for 2 minutes, or until they begin to brown.

5 Arrange a handful of salad leaves on each plate and top with a large spoonful of the apple and beetroot mixture. Sprinkle with the pecans and serve.

goat's cheese tarts

MAKES 12

butter, for greasing

400 g/14 oz packet ready-rolled puff pastry

1 tbsp plain flour

1 egg, beaten

3 tbsp onion or tomato relish

three x 115-g/4-oz goat's cheese logs, sliced

extra virgin olive oil, for drizzling

pepper

1 Preheat the oven to 200°C/400°F/Gas Mark 6 and grease several baking trays.

2 Cut out as many 7.5-cm/3-inch rounds as possible from the pastry on a lightly floured work surface.

3 Place the rounds on the baking trays and press gently about 2.5 cm/1 inch from the edge of each with a 5-cm/2-inch pastry cutter.

4 Brush the rounds with beaten egg and prick with a fork. Top each circle with a little relish and a slice of goat's cheese. Drizzle with oil and sprinkle over a little pepper.

5 Bake for 8–10 minutes, or until the pastry is crisp and the cheese is bubbling. Serve warm.

nachos with chillies & olives

SERVES 4

1 kg/2 lb 4 oz tortilla chips

6 tbsp chopped pickled jalapeño chillies

115 g/4 oz black olives, stoned and sliced

450 g/1 lb Cheddar cheese, grated

dipping sauce

1 Preheat the oven to 180°C/350°F/Gas Mark 4. Spread out the tortilla chips in a large ovenproof dish.

2 Sprinkle the chillies, olives and grated cheese evenly over the tortilla chips and bake for 12–15 minutes, or until the cheese is melted and bubbling. Serve immediately with a dipping sauce of your choice.

quinoa with roasted vegetables

SERVES 2

2 peppers (any colour), deseeded and cut into chunky pieces

1 large courgette, cut into chunks

1 small fennel bulb, cut into slim wedges

1 tbsp olive oil

2 tsp very finely chopped fresh rosemary leaves

1 tsp chopped fresh thyme leaves

100 g/3½ oz quinoa

350 ml/12 fl oz vegetable stock

2 garlic cloves, peeled and crushed

3 tbsp chopped fresh flat leaf parsley

40 g/1½ oz pine nuts, toasted

salt and pepper

1 Preheat the oven to 200°C/400°F/Gas Mark 6. Place the peppers, courgette and fennel in a roasting tin large enough to hold the vegetables in a single layer.

2 Drizzle the olive oil over the vegetables and scatter with the rosemary and thyme. Season well with salt and pepper and mix well with clean hands. Roast for 25–30 minutes until tender and lightly charred.

3 Meanwhile, place the quinoa, stock and garlic in a saucepan. Bring to the boil, cover and simmer for 12–15 minutes until tender and most of the stock has been absorbed.

4 Remove the vegetables from the oven. Tip the quinoa into the roasting tin. Add the parsley and pine nuts and toss together. Serve warm or cold.

grilled halloumi with herbed couscous

SERVES 4

**450 g/1 lb halloumi cheese,
cut into 5-mm/¼-inch
slices**

4 tbsp chilli oil

herbed couscous

**400 ml/14 fl oz hot
vegetable stock**

225 g/8 oz couscous

**2 tbsp chopped fresh mixed
herbs**

2 tsp lemon juice

1 tbsp olive oil

1 Preheat the grill to high and line the grill rack with foil. Put the cheese slices in a bowl, pour over the chilli oil and toss well to coat the cheese.

2 Place the cheese on the grill rack and cook under the grill for 2–3 minutes on each side until golden.

3 Meanwhile, stir the hot stock into the couscous in a large bowl. Cover and leave to stand for 5 minutes.

4 Stir the herbs, lemon juice and olive oil into the couscous. Serve with the grilled halloumi cheese on top.

baked chilli cheese sandwiches

MAKES 4

350 g/12 oz grated cheese, such as Cheddar

115 g/4 oz butter, softened, plus extra to finish

4 fresh green chillies, deseeded and chopped

½ tsp ground cumin

8 thick slices bread

1 Preheat the oven to 190°C/375°F/Gas Mark 5. Mix together the cheese and butter in a bowl until creamy then add the chillies and cumin.

2 Spread this mixture over 4 slices of bread and top with the remaining slices.

3 Spread the outside of the sandwiches with extra butter and bake for 8–10 minutes until crisp. Serve.

cheesy baked courgettes

SERVES 4

4 medium courgettes

2 tbsp extra virgin olive oil

115 g/4 oz mozzarella cheese, sliced thinly

2 large tomatoes, deseeded and diced

2 tsp fresh basil or oregano, chopped

1 Preheat the oven to 200°C/400°F/Gas Mark 6. Slice the courgettes lengthways into 4 strips each. Brush with oil and place on an ovenproof tray.

2 Bake the courgettes in the oven for 10 minutes without letting them get too floppy.

3 Remove the courgettes from the oven. Arrange slices of cheese on top and sprinkle with diced tomato and basil. Return to the oven for 5 minutes or until the cheese melts.

4 Remove the courgettes from the oven and transfer carefully to serving plates, or serve straight from the baking dish.

thai tofu cakes with chilli dip

SERVES 8

300 g/10½ oz firm tofu,
drained weight,
coarsely grated

1 lemon grass stalk,
finely chopped

2 garlic cloves, chopped

2.5-cm/1-inch piece
fresh ginger, grated

2 kaffir lime leaves,
finely chopped (optional)

2 shallots, finely chopped

2 fresh red chillies,
deseeded and finely
chopped

4 tbsp chopped fresh
coriander

90 g/3¼ oz gluten-free
plain flour,
plus extra for flouring

½ tsp salt

corn oil, for cooking

chilli dip

3 tbsp white distilled
vinegar

2 spring onions,
finely sliced

1 tbsp caster sugar

2 fresh chillies, chopped

2 tbsp chopped fresh
coriander

pinch of salt

1 To make the chilli dip, mix all the ingredients together in a small serving bowl and set aside.

2 Mix the tofu with the lemon grass, garlic, ginger, lime leaves, if using, shallots, chillies and coriander in a mixing bowl. Stir in the flour and salt to make a coarse, sticky paste. Cover and chill in the refrigerator for 1 hour to let the mixture firm up slightly.

3 Form the mixture into 8 large walnut-sized balls and, using floured hands, flatten into circles. Heat enough oil to cover the bottom of a large, heavy-based frying pan over medium heat. Cook the cakes in 2 batches, turning halfway through, for 4–6 minutes, or until golden brown. Drain on kitchen paper and serve warm with the chilli dip.

sweet potato, leek & feta patties

SERVES 4

1 whole garlic bulb

115 g/4 oz sweet potatoes, peeled and cut into chunks

175 g/6 oz carrots, peeled and chopped

115 g/4 oz leeks, trimmed and finely chopped

55 g/2 oz feta cheese, crumbled

1–2 tsp Tabasco sauce, or to taste

1 tbsp chopped fresh coriander

pepper

fresh herbs or salad, to garnish

tomato ketchup, to serve (optional)

1 Preheat the oven to 190°C/375°F/Gas Mark 5. Break the garlic bulb open, place in a small roasting tin and roast for 20 minutes, or until soft. Remove and when cool enough to handle, squeeze out the roasted garlic flesh.

2 Cook the sweet potatoes and carrots in a large saucepan of boiling water for 15 minutes, or until soft. Drain and mash, then mix in the roasted garlic flesh.

3 Add the leeks, feta cheese, Tabasco sauce, coriander and pepper to the sweet potato mixture. Cover and leave to chill in the refrigerator for at least 30 minutes.

4 Using slightly dampened hands, shape the sweet potato mixture into 8 small round patties and place on a non-stick baking sheet. Bake for 15–20 minutes, or until piping hot. Garnish with fresh herbs or salad and serve with tomato ketchup, if using.

tomato ratatouille

4 sprays olive oil

1 onion, cut into small wedges

2–4 garlic cloves, chopped

1 small aubergine, trimmed and chopped

1 small red pepper, deseeded and chopped

1 small yellow pepper, deseeded and chopped

1 courgette, trimmed and chopped

2 tbsp tomato purée

3 tbsp water

115 g/4 oz mushrooms, sliced if large

225 g/8 oz ripe tomatoes, chopped

pepper

1 tbsp shredded fresh basil, to garnish

25 g/1 oz Parmesan-style vegetarian cheese, freshly shaved, to serve

1 Heat the oil in a heavy-based saucepan, add the onion, garlic and aubergine and cook, stirring frequently for 3 minutes.

2 Add the peppers and courgette. Mix together the tomato purée and water in a small bowl and stir into the pan. Bring to the boil, cover with a lid, reduce the heat to a simmer and cook for 10 minutes.

3 Add the mushrooms and chopped tomatoes with pepper to taste and continue to simmer for 12–15 minutes, stirring occasionally, until the vegetables are tender.

4 Divide the ratatouille between 4 warmed bowls, garnish each with shredded basil and serve with freshly shaved Parmesan-style vegetarian cheese to sprinkle over.

spicy stuffed peppers

SERVES 4

4 assorted coloured peppers

3 sprays olive oil

1 onion, finely chopped

2 garlic cloves, chopped

2.5-cm/1-inch piece fresh ginger, peeled and grated

1–2 fresh serrano chillies, deseeded and chopped

1 tsp ground cumin

1 tsp ground coriander

85 g/3 oz cooked brown basmati rice

1 large carrot, about 115 g/ 4 oz, peeled and grated

1 large courgette, about 85 g/3 oz, trimmed and grated

25 g/1 oz ready-to-eat dried apricots, finely chopped

1 tbsp chopped fresh coriander

150 ml/5 fl oz water

pepper

fresh herbs, to garnish

1 Preheat the oven to 190°C/375°F/Gas Mark 5. Cut the tops off the peppers and reserve. Discard the seeds from each pepper. Place the peppers in a large bowl and cover with boiling water. Leave to soak for 10 minutes then drain and reserve.

2 Heat a non-stick frying pan and spray with the oil. Add the onion, garlic, ginger and chillies and sauté for 3 minutes, stirring frequently. Sprinkle in the ground spices and continue to cook for a further 2 minutes.

3 Remove the pan from the heat and stir in the rice, carrot, courgette, apricots, chopped coriander and pepper to taste. Stir well, then use to stuff the peppers.

4 Place the stuffed peppers in an ovenproof dish large enough to allow the peppers to stand upright. Put the reserved tops in position. Pour the water around their bases, cover loosely with the lid or foil and bake for 25–30 minutes, or until piping hot. Serve garnished with herbs.

stir-fried rice with green vegetables

SERVES 4

225 g/8 oz jasmine rice

2 tbsp vegetable or peanut oil

1 tbsp green curry paste

6 spring onions, sliced

2 garlic cloves, crushed

1 courgette, cut into thin sticks

115 g/4 oz French beans

175 g/6 oz asparagus, trimmed

3–4 fresh Thai basil leaves

1 Cook the rice in lightly salted boiling water for 12–15 minutes, drain well, then cool thoroughly and chill.

2 Heat the oil in a wok and stir-fry the curry paste for 1 minute. Add the spring onions and garlic and stir-fry for 1 minute.

3 Add the courgette, beans and asparagus and stir-fry for 3–4 minutes, until just tender. Break up the rice and add it to the wok. Cook, stirring constantly for 2–3 minutes, until the rice is hot. Stir in the basil and serve immediately.

falafel burgers

SERVES 4

**two x 400-g/14-oz cans
chickpeas, drained and
rinsed**

1 small onion, chopped

zest and juice of 1 lime

2 tsp ground coriander

2 tsp ground cumin

6 tbsp plain flour

4 tbsp olive oil

**4 sprigs fresh basil,
to garnish**

tomato salsa, to serve

1 Put the chickpeas, onion, lime zest and juice and the spices into a food processor and process to a coarse paste.

2 Tip the mixture out onto a clean work surface or chopping board and shape into 4 burgers.

3 Spread the flour out on a large flat plate and use to coat the burgers.

4 Heat the oil in a large frying pan, add the burgers and cook for 2 minutes on each side until crisp. Garnish with basil and serve with tomato salsa.

open rösti omelette

SERVES 4

55 g/2 oz old potatoes, peeled and grated

1 onion, grated

2 garlic cloves, crushed

1 carrot, about 115 g/4 oz, peeled and grated

4 sprays olive oil

1 yellow pepper, peeled and thinly sliced

1 courgette, about 85 g/ 3 oz, trimmed and thinly sliced

85 g/3 oz cherry tomatoes, halved

2 eggs

3 egg whites

1 tbsp snipped fresh chives

pepper

fresh rocket leaves, to garnish

1 Put the grated potatoes into a large bowl and cover with cold water. Leave for 15 minutes then drain, rinse thoroughly and dry on absorbent kitchen paper or a clean tea towel. Mix with the grated onion, garlic and carrot.

2 Heat a heavy-based non-stick frying pan and spray with the oil. Add the potato, onion, garlic and carrot mixture and cook over a low heat for 5 minutes, pressing the vegetables down firmly with a spatula. Add the peeled pepper and courgette slices. Cover with a lid or crumpled piece of foil and cook very gently, stirring occasionally, for 5 minutes.

3 Add the halved cherry tomatoes and cook for a further 2 minutes, or until the vegetables are tender.

4 Beat together the whole eggs, egg whites, chives and pepper to taste in a bowl. Pour over the vegetable mixture and cook for 4–5 minutes, stirring the egg from the sides of the pan towards the centre, until the vegetables are tender and the eggs are set. Serve immediately, garnished with rocket leaves.

courgette, carrot & tomato frittata

SERVES 4

2 sprays olive oil

**1 onion,
cut into small wedges**

1–2 garlic cloves, crushed

2 eggs

2 egg whites

**1 courgette, about 85 g/
3 oz, trimmed and grated**

**2 carrots, about 115 g/4 oz,
peeled and grated**

2 tomatoes, chopped

pepper

**1 tbsp shredded fresh basil,
for sprinkling**

1 Heat the oil in a large non-stick frying pan, add the onion and garlic and sauté for 5 minutes, stirring frequently. Beat the eggs and egg whites in a bowl then pour into the pan. Using a spatula or fork, pull the egg mixture from the sides of the pan into the centre, allowing the uncooked egg to take its place.

2 Once the base has set lightly, add the grated courgette and carrots with the tomatoes. Add pepper to taste and continue to cook over a low heat until the eggs are set to personal preference.

3 Sprinkle with the shredded basil, cut the frittata into quarters and serve.

leek & goat's cheese crêpes

MAKES 8

25 g/1 oz unsalted butter

½ tbsp sunflower oil

200 g/7 oz leeks, halved, rinsed and finely shredded

freshly grated nutmeg, to taste

1 tbsp finely snipped fresh chives

8 Savoury Crêpes

85 g/3 oz soft goat's cheese, rind removed if necessary, chopped

salt and pepper

1 Preheat the oven to 200°C/400°F/Gas Mark 6. Melt the butter with the oil in a heavy-based saucepan with a lid over a medium–high heat. Add the leeks and stir around so that they are well coated. Stir in salt and pepper to taste. Add a few gratings of nutmeg, then cover the leeks with a sheet of wet greaseproof paper and cover the pan. Reduce the heat to very low and leave the leeks to sweat for 5–7 minutes until very tender, but not brown. Stir in the chives, then taste and adjust the seasoning if necessary.

2 Put 1 crêpe on the work surface and put one eighth of the leeks on the crêpe, top with one eighth of the cheese, then fold the crêpe into a square parcel or simply roll it around the filling. Place the stuffed crêpe on a baking tray, then continue to fill and fold or roll the remaining crêpes.

3 Put the baking tray in the oven and bake for 5 minutes, or until the crêpes are hot and the cheese starts to melt. Serve hot.

VARIATION

Replace the goat's cheese with your favourite cheese to add a different flavour. For a stronger cheese taste, sprinkle some grated cheese or small chunks over the top of the crêpes before baking.

3

Marvellous Mains

tofu stir-fry

SERVES 4

2 tbsp sunflower or olive oil

350 g/12 oz firm tofu, cubed

225 g/8 oz pak choi, roughly chopped

1 garlic clove, chopped

4 tbsp sweet chilli sauce

2 tbsp light soy sauce

1 Heat 1 tablespoon of oil in a wok, add the tofu in batches and stir-fry for 2–3 minutes until golden. Remove and set aside.

2 Add the pak choi to the wok and stir-fry for a few seconds until tender and wilted. Remove and set aside.

3 Add the remaining oil to the wok, then add the garlic and stir-fry for 30 seconds.

4 Stir in the chilli sauce and soy sauce and bring to the boil.

5 Return the tofu and pak choi to the wok and toss gently until coated in the sauce. Serve immediately.

summer stir-fry

SERVES 4

115 g/4 oz French beans

115 g/4 oz mangetout

115 g/4 oz carrots

**115 g/4 oz asparagus
spears**

½ red pepper

½ orange pepper

½ yellow pepper

2 celery sticks

3 spring onions

**2 tbsp groundnut or
sunflower oil**

**1 tsp finely chopped
fresh ginger**

**2 garlic cloves,
finely chopped**

115 g/4 oz broccoli florets

salt

Chinese chives, to garnish

1 Slice the French beans, mangetout, carrots, asparagus, peppers, celery and spring onions and reserve. Heat half the oil in a preheated wok or heavy-based frying pan. Add the ginger and garlic and stir-fry for a few seconds, then add the French beans and stir-fry for 2 minutes.

2 Add the mangetout, stir-fry for 1 minute, then add the broccoli florets, carrots and asparagus and stir-fry for 2 minutes.

3 Add the remaining oil, the peppers, celery and spring onions and stir-fry for a further 2–3 minutes, or until all the vegetables are crisp and tender. Season to taste with salt and serve immediately, garnished with Chinese chives.

noodle stir-fry

SERVES 2

140 g/5 oz flat rice noodles

6 tbsp soy sauce

2 tbsp lemon juice

1 tsp granulated sugar

½ tsp cornflour

1 tbsp vegetable oil

2 tsp grated fresh ginger

2 garlic cloves, chopped

4–5 spring onions, trimmed and sliced

2 tbsp rice wine or dry sherry

200 g/7 oz canned water chestnuts, drained and sliced

1 Put the noodles in a large bowl and cover with boiling water. Leave to stand for 4 minutes. Drain and rinse under cold running water.

2 Mix together the soy sauce, lemon juice, sugar and cornflour in small bowl.

3 Heat the oil in a wok, add the ginger and garlic and stir-fry for 1 minute. Add the spring onions and stir-fry for 3 minutes.

4 Add the rice wine or dry sherry, followed by the soy sauce mixture and cook for 1 minute.

5 Stir in the water chestnuts and noodles and cook for a further 1–2 minutes, or until heated through. Serve immediately.

bean burgers

SERVES 4

**1 tbsp sunflower oil,
plus extra for brushing**

1 onion, finely chopped

**1 garlic clove,
finely chopped**

1 tsp ground coriander

1 tsp ground cumin

**115 g/4 oz white
mushrooms,
finely chopped**

**425 g/15 oz canned borlotti
or red kidney beans,
drained and rinsed**

**2 tbsp chopped fresh
flat-leaf parsley**

plain flour, for dusting

salt and pepper

**hamburger buns and salad,
to serve**

1 Heat the oil in a heavy-based frying pan over medium heat. Add the onion and cook, stirring frequently, for 5 minutes, or until softened. Add the garlic, coriander and cumin and cook, stirring, for a further minute. Add the mushrooms and cook, stirring frequently, for 4–5 minutes until all the liquid has evaporated. Transfer to a bowl.

2 Put the beans in a small bowl and mash with a fork. Stir into the mushroom mixture with the parsley and season with salt and pepper.

3 Preheat the grill to medium–high. Divide the mixture equally into 4 portions, dust lightly with flour and shape into flat, round burgers. Brush with oil and cook under the grill for 4–5 minutes on each side. Serve in hamburger buns with salad.

vegetable chilli

SERVES 4

1 aubergine, cut into
2.5-cm/1-inch slices

1 tbsp olive oil,
plus extra for brushing

1 large red onion,
chopped finely

2 red or yellow peppers,
deseeded and chopped
finely

3–4 garlic cloves, finely
chopped or crushed

800 g/1 lb 12 oz canned
chopped tomatoes

1 tbsp mild chilli powder

½ tsp ground cumin

½ tsp dried oregano

2 small courgettes,
quartered lengthways
and sliced

400 g/14 oz canned kidney
beans, drained and
rinsed

450 ml/16 fl oz water

1 tbsp tomato purée

6 spring onions,
chopped finely

115 g/4 oz Cheddar cheese,
grated

salt and pepper

1 Brush the aubergine slices on one side with olive oil. Heat half the oil in a large, heavy-based frying pan over a medium-high heat. Add the aubergine slices, oiled-side up, and cook for 5–6 minutes, or until browned on one side. Turn the slices over, cook on the other side until browned and transfer to a plate. Cut into bite-sized pieces.

2 Heat the remaining oil in a large saucepan over a medium heat. Add the onion and peppers and cook, stirring occasionally, for 3–4 minutes, or until the onion is just softened, but not browned.

3 Add the garlic and cook for a further 2–3 minutes, or until the onion is beginning to colour.

4 Add the tomatoes, chilli powder, cumin and oregano. Season to taste with salt and pepper. Bring just to the boil, reduce the heat, cover and simmer gently for 15 minutes.

5 Add the courgettes, aubergine pieces and kidney beans. Stir in the water and the tomato purée. Return to the boil, then cover and continue simmering for 45 minutes, or until the vegetables are tender. Taste and adjust the seasoning if necessary. Ladle into warmed serving bowls and top with spring onions and cheese.

leek & spinach pie

SERVES 6–8

225 g/8 oz puff pastry

2 tbsp unsalted butter

2 leeks, sliced finely

225 g/8 oz spinach, chopped

2 eggs

300 ml/10 fl oz double cream

pinch of dried thyme

salt and pepper

1 Preheat the oven to 180°C/350°F/Gas Mark 4. Roll the pastry into a rectangle about 25 x 30 cm/10 x 12 inches. Leave to rest for 5 minutes, then press into a 20 x 25 cm/ 8 x 10 inch pie dish. Do not trim the overhang. Cover the pastry with aluminium foil and refrigerate.

2 Melt the butter in a large frying pan over a medium heat. Add the leeks, stir and cook gently for 5 minutes, or until soft. Add the spinach and cook for 3 minutes, or until soft. Leave to cool.

3 Beat the eggs in a bowl. Stir in the cream and season with thyme and salt and pepper. Remove the pastry case and uncover. Spread the cooked vegetables over the base and pour in the egg mixture.

4 Place on a baking sheet and bake for 30 minutes, or until set. Remove the pie from the oven and leave to rest for 10 minutes before serving. Serve directly from the flan dish.

cheese & vegetable tart

SERVES 4

butter, for greasing

350 g/12 oz ready-made shortcrust pastry, thawed if frozen

plain flour, for dusting

280 g/10 oz mixed frozen vegetables

150 ml/5 fl oz double cream

115 g/4 oz Cheddar cheese, grated

salt and pepper

1 Preheat the oven to 200°C/400°C/Gas Mark 6. Lightly grease a 23-cm/9-inch loose-based quiche tin. Roll out the dough on a lightly floured work surface and use to line the tin. Prick the base and chill in the refrigerator for 30 minutes.

2 Line the pastry case with foil and half-fill with baking beans. Place the tin on a baking sheet and bake for 15–20 minutes, or until just firm. Remove the beans and foil, return the pastry case to the oven and bake for a further 5–7 minutes until golden. Remove the pastry case from the oven and leave to cool in the tin.

3 Meanwhile, cook the frozen vegetables in a saucepan of salted boiling water. Drain and leave to cool.

4 When ready to cook, preheat the oven again to 200°C/400°F/Gas Mark 6. Mix the cooked vegetables and cream together and season with salt and pepper. Spoon the mixture evenly into the pastry case and sprinkle with the cheese. Bake for 15 minutes, or until the cheese has melted and is turning golden. Serve hot or cold.

mushroom & onion quiche

SERVES 4

butter, for greasing

**100g pre-bought
shortcrust pastry**

**plain flour,
for dusting**

filling

55 g/2 oz unsalted butter

**3 red onions,
halved and sliced**

**350 g/12 oz mixed wild
mushrooms, such as
ceps, chanterelles and
morels**

2 tsp chopped fresh thyme

1 egg

2 egg yolks

**100 ml/3½ fl oz double
cream**

salt and pepper

1 Preheat the oven to 190°C/375°F/Gas Mark 5. Lightly grease a 23-cm/9-inch loose-based quiche tin. Roll out the dough on a lightly floured work surface and use to line the tin. Line the pastry case with baking paper and fill with baking beans. Chill in the refrigerator for 30 minutes. Bake in the preheated oven for 25 minutes. Remove the paper and beans and cool on a wire rack. Reduce the oven temperature to 180°C/350°F/Gas Mark 4.

2 To make the filling, melt the butter in a large, heavy-based frying pan over a very low heat. Add the onions, cover and cook, stirring occasionally, for 20 minutes. Add the mushrooms and thyme and cook, stirring occasionally, for a further 10 minutes. Spoon into the pastry case and put the tin on a baking tray.

3 Lightly beat the egg, egg yolks, cream and salt and pepper to taste in a bowl. Pour over the mushroom mixture. Bake in the oven for 10–15 minutes, or until the filling is set and golden. Serve hot or at room temperature.

caramelized onion tart

SERVES 4–6

100 g/3½ oz unsalted butter

600 g/1 lb 5 oz onions, thinly sliced

2 eggs

100 ml/3½ fl oz double cream

100 g/3½ oz grated Gruyère cheese

20 cm/8 inch baked pastry case

100 g/3½ oz grated Parmesan-style vegetarian cheese

salt and pepper

1 Preheat the oven to 190°C/375°F/Gas Mark 5. Melt the butter over a medium heat in a heavy frying pan. Stir in the onions and cook until they are well browned and caramelized. (This will take up to 30 minutes, depending on the width of the pan.) Stir frequently to avoid burning. Remove the onions from the pan and set aside.

2 Beat the eggs in a large mixing bowl, stir in the cream and season with salt and pepper. Add the Gruyère and mix well. Mix in the cooked onions.

3 Pour the egg and onion mixture into the baked pastry case, sprinkle with Parmesan-style vegetarian cheese and place on an ovenproof tray. Bake for 15–20 minutes or until the filling has set and begun to brown.

4 Remove from the oven and leave to rest for at least 10 minutes. The tart can be served hot or left to cool to room temperature.

bubble & squeak

SERVES 4

450 g/1 lb floury potatoes, peeled and diced

2 tbsp milk

55 g/2 oz butter, plus extra for greasing

225 g/8 oz green cabbage, shredded

225 g/8 oz carrots, sliced thinly

1 medium onion, chopped

55 g/2 oz Cheddar cheese, grated

salt and pepper

1 Preheat the oven to 190°C/375°F/Gas Mark 5. Cook the potatoes in salted water for 10 minutes, or until soft. Drain well and turn into a large mixing bowl. Mash until smooth. Beat with the milk, half of the butter and salt and pepper to taste.

2 Cook the cabbage and carrots separately in salted boiling water for 5 minutes. Drain well. Mix the cabbage into the potatoes. Melt the remaining butter in a small frying pan and cook the onion over a medium heat until soft but not brown.

3 Spread a layer of mashed potatoes in the bottom of a greased shallow ovenproof dish. Layer onions on top, then carrots. Repeat to use up all the ingredients, finishing with a layer of potato.

4 Sprinkle the grated cheese on top, place the dish in the oven and bake for 45 minutes, or until the top is golden and crusty. Remove from the oven and serve immediately.

leek & egg mornay

SERVES 4

2 tbsp butter

**4 leeks, trimmed and
sliced**

**8 hard-boiled eggs,
shelled and quartered**

55 g/2 oz butter

55 g/2 oz plain flour

300 ml/10 fl oz milk

**55 g/2 oz Cheddar or
emmenthal cheese,
grated**

1 tsp wholegrain mustard

cayenne pepper (optional)

salt and pepper

1 Preheat the grill to high. Melt the butter in a frying pan over medium heat, add the leeks and cook. Remove when soft and put in a baking dish. Arrange the egg quarters on top and season to taste.

2 Meanwhile, melt the butter in a small pan over a medium heat. Gradually add the flour, stirring constantly until it has been absorbed. Still stirring, slowly add the milk, until blended. Bring the sauce to the boil, reduce the heat and simmer, stirring, until it thickens. Add the cheese, mustard and cayenne pepper (if using), stirring until well blended. Pour the sauce over the eggs and leeks.

3 Put the dish under the grill for 2–3 minutes. Serve when bubbling.

butternut squash & mushroom risotto

SERVES 4

2 tbsp olive oil

1 large onion, finely chopped

6 sage leaves, finely chopped

2 tsp chopped fresh thyme leaves

700 g/1 lb 9 oz butternut squash, peeled, deseeded and cut into 2 cm/¾ inch chunks

225 g/8 oz chestnut mushrooms, sliced

300 ml/10 fl oz vegetable stock

200 ml/7 fl oz dry white wine

350 g/12 oz risotto rice

55 g/2 oz grated Parmesan-style vegetarian cheese

salt and pepper

crispy fried sage leaves, to garnish

1 Preheat the oven to 200°C/400°F/Gas Mark 6. Heat the oil in a large saucepan. Add the onion, sage and thyme. Cover and cook over a low heat for 5 minutes until the onion turns translucent.

2 Stir in the butternut squash, mushrooms, stock and wine. Bring to the boil, then remove from the heat and ladle everything in the pan into a large ovenproof casserole. Stir in the rice.

3 Cover the casserole with a tight fitting lid and bake for 40–45 minutes until the rice and vegetables are tender. Stir in half the cheese, then season with salt and pepper. Serve immediately sprinkled with the remaining cheese and fried sage leaves to garnish.

mushroom & cauliflower cheese crumble

SERVES 4

1 medium cauliflower

55 g/2 oz butter

115 g/4 oz button mushrooms, sliced

salt and pepper

topping

115 g/4 oz dry breadcrumbs

2 tbsp grated Parmesan-style vegetarian cheese

1 tsp dried oregano

1 tsp dried parsley

2 tbsp butter

1 Preheat the oven to 230°C/450°F/Gas Mark 8. Bring a large pan of salted water to the boil. Break the cauliflower into small florets and cook in the boiling water for 3 minutes. Remove from the heat, drain well and transfer to a large shallow ovenproof dish.

2 Melt the butter in a small frying pan over a medium heat. Add the sliced mushrooms, stir to coat and cook gently for 3 minutes. Remove from the heat and add to the cauliflower. Season with salt and pepper.

3 For the topping, combine the breadcrumbs, cheese and herbs in a small mixing bowl, then sprinkle the crumbs over the vegetables.

4 Dice the butter and dot over the crumbs. Place the dish in the oven and bake for 15 minutes, or until the crumbs are golden brown and crisp. Serve from the cooking dish.

pizza turnovers

SERVES 4

2 x quantities ready-made pizza dough

plain flour, for dusting

filling

2 tbsp olive oil, plus extra for oiling

1 red onion, thinly sliced

1 garlic clove, finely chopped

400 g/14 oz canned chopped tomatoes

55 g/2 oz stoned black olives

200 g/7 oz mozzarella cheese, drained and diced

1 tbsp chopped fresh oregano

salt and pepper

1 Preheat the oven to 200°C/400°F/Gas Mark 6. To make the filling, heat the olive oil in a frying pan. Add the onion and garlic and cook over a low heat, stirring occasionally, for 5 minutes, until softened. Add the tomatoes and cook, stirring occasionally, for a further 5 minutes. Stir in the olives and season to taste with salt and pepper. Remove the frying pan from the heat.

2 Divide the dough into 4 pieces. Roll out each piece on a lightly floured surface to form a 20-cm/8-inch round.

3 Divide the tomato mixture between the rounds, spreading it over half of each almost to the edge. Top with the cheese and sprinkle with the oregano. Brush the edge of each round with a little water and fold over the uncovered sides. Press the edges to seal. Bake for about 15 minutes, until golden and crisp. Remove from the oven and leave to stand for 2 minutes, then transfer to warmed plates and serve.

cheese &
tomato pizza

SERVES 4–6

pizza dough

oil, for brushing

plain flour, for dusting

**1 quantity ready-made
pizza dough**

topping

6 tomatoes, thinly sliced

**175 g/6 oz mozzarella
cheese, drained and
thinly sliced**

2 tbsp shredded fresh basil

2 tbsp olive oil

salt and pepper

1 Preheat the oven to 230°C/450°F/Gas Mark 8. Brush a baking tray with a little oil. Roll out the dough on a lightly floured surface to a 25-cm/10-inch round. Place on the baking sheet and push up the edge a little. Cover and let stand in a warm place for 10 minutes.

2 For the topping, arrange the tomato and mozzarella slices over the pizza base. Season to taste with salt and pepper, sprinkle with the basil and drizzle with the oil. Bake in the preheated oven for 20–25 minutes, until golden brown. Cut into slices and serve immediately.

SERVES 2–4

**2 tbsp olive oil,
plus extra for brushing
and drizzling**

**1 quantity ready-made
pizza dough**

plain flour, for dusting

350 g/12 oz spinach

1 onion, thinly sliced

6 tbsp ricotta cheese

**½ tsp freshly grated
nutmeg**

2 tbsp pine kernels

**115 g/4 oz Fontina cheese,
sliced thinly**

salt and pepper

1 Preheat the oven to 220°C/425°F/Gas Mark 7. Brush a baking sheet with oil.

2 Roll out the dough on a lightly floured surface to a 25-cm/10-inch round. Place on the baking sheet and push up the edge a little. Cover and let stand in a warm place for 10 minutes.

3 Wash the spinach in cold water and dry well. Heat the oil in a pan, add the onion and cook until soft and translucent. Add the spinach and cook, stirring, until just wilted. Remove the pan from the heat and drain off any liquid.

4 Spread the ricotta cheese evenly over the pizza base, then cover with the spinach and onion mixture. Sprinkle over the nutmeg and pine kernels and season to taste with salt and pepper. Top with the slices of Fontina and drizzle with olive oil. Bake in the oven for 20–30 minutes, until golden and sizzling. Serve immediately.

mozzarella gnocchi

SERVES 2–4

butter, for greasing

450 g/1 lb packet potato gnocchi

200 ml/7 fl oz double cream

225 g/8 oz firm mozzarella cheese, grated or chopped

salt and pepper

1 Preheat the grill and grease a large baking dish. Cook the gnocchi in a large saucepan of boiling salted water for about 3 minutes, or according to the packet instructions. Drain and put into the prepared baking dish.

2 Season the cream with salt and pepper and drizzle over the gnocchi. Scatter over the cheese and cook under the grill for a few minutes until the top is browned and bubbling. Serve immediately.

vegetarian lasagne

SERVES 4

40 g/1½ oz dried porcini mushrooms

2 tbsp olive oil

1 onion, finely chopped

400 g/14 oz canned chopped tomatoes

55 g/2 oz butter, plus extra for greasing

450 g/1 lb button mushrooms, thinly sliced

1 garlic clove, finely chopped

1 tbsp lemon juice

½ tsp Dijon mustard

¾ quantity of cheese sauce, made with Cheddar cheese

6 sheets no-precook lasagne

55 g/2 oz freshly grated Parmesan-style vegetarian cheese

salt and pepper

1 Preheat the oven to 200°C/400°F/Gas Mark 6. Place the porcini mushrooms in a small bowl, cover with boiling water and leave to soak for 30 minutes. Meanwhile, heat the oil in a small frying pan. Add the onion and cook, stirring occasionally, for 5 minutes, or until softened. Add the tomatoes and cook, stirring frequently, for 7–8 minutes. Season with salt and pepper and reserve.

2 Drain and slice the porcini mushrooms. Melt half the butter in a large, heavy-based frying pan. Add the porcini and button mushrooms and cook until they begin to release their juices. Add the garlic and lemon juice and season to taste with salt and pepper. Cook over a low heat, stirring occasionally, until almost all the liquid has evaporated.

3 Lightly grease an ovenproof dish with butter. Stir the mustard into the cheese sauce, then spread a layer over the base of the dish. Place a layer of lasagne sheets on top, cover with the mushrooms, another layer of sauce, another layer of lasagne, the tomato mixture and finally, another layer of sauce. Sprinkle with the Parmesan-style vegetarian cheese and dot with the remaining butter. Bake in the preheated oven for 20 minutes. Leave to stand for 5 minutes before serving.

pasta with tomatoes & spinach

SERVES 4

450 g/1 lb dried orecchiette or other pasta shapes

3 tbsp olive oil

225 g/8 oz fresh baby spinach leaves, tough stalks removed

450 g/1 lb cherry tomatoes, halved

Parmesan-style vegetarian cheese, grated (optional)

salt and pepper

1 Bring a large saucepan of lightly salted water to the boil. Add the pasta, bring back to the boil and cook for 10–12 minutes, until tender but still firm to the bite.

2 Heat the oil in a saucepan, add the spinach and tomatoes and cook, gently stirring occasionally, for 2–3 minutes, or until the spinach has wilted and the tomatoes are heated through but not disintegrating.

3 Drain the pasta and add it to the pan of vegetables. Toss gently, season with salt and pepper, sprinkle over some Parmesan-style vegetarian cheese, if using, and serve immediately.

double cheese
macaroni

SERVES 4

225 g/8 oz dried macaroni

250 g/9 oz ricotta cheese

1½ tbsp wholegrain mustard

**3 tbsp snipped fresh chives,
plus extra to garnish**

**200 g/7 oz cherry tomatoes,
halved**

**100 g/3½ oz sun-dried
tomatoes in oil,
drained and chopped**

butter or oil, for greasing

**100 g/3½ oz Cheddar
cheese, grated**

salt and pepper

1 Preheat the grill to high. Bring a large saucepan of lightly salted water to the boil. Add the macaroni, bring back to the boil and cook for 10–12 minutes, until tender but still firm to the bite. Drain.

2 Mix the ricotta with the mustard, chives and salt and pepper to taste. Stir in the macaroni, cherry tomatoes and sundried tomatoes.

3 Grease a 1.7-litre/3-pint shallow ovenproof dish. Spoon in the macaroni mixture, spreading evenly.

4 Sprinkle the Cheddar cheese over the macaroni mixture and cook under the preheated grill for 4–5 minutes, until golden and bubbling. Serve the macaroni sprinkled with extra chives.

pasta with olive sauce

SERVES 2–4

350 g/12 oz fresh pasta shapes

½ tsp salt

6 tbsp olive oil

½ tsp freshly grated nutmeg

½ tsp black pepper

1 garlic clove, crushed

2 tbsp tapenade

85g/3 oz black or green olives, stoned and sliced

1 tbsp chopped fresh parsley, to garnish (optional)

salt

1 Bring a large saucepan of lightly salted water to the boil. Add the pasta, bring back to the boil and cook for 4–6 minutes, until tender but still firm to the bite.

2 Meanwhile, put ½ teaspoon of salt with the oil, nutmeg, pepper, garlic, tapenade and olives in another saucepan and heat slowly but don't allow to boil. Cover and leave to stand for 3–4 minutes.

3 Drain the pasta and return to the saucepan. Add the flavoured oil and heat gently for 1–2 minutes. Serve immediately garnished with chopped parsley, if using.

chilli broccoli pasta

SERVES 4

225 g/8 oz dry penne or macaroni

225 g/8 oz broccoli

50 ml/2 fl oz extra virgin olive oil

2 large garlic cloves, chopped

2 fresh red chillies, deseeded and diced

8 cherry tomatoes (optional)

small handful of fresh basil or parsley, to garnish

salt

1 Bring a large saucepan of lightly salted water to the boil. Add the pasta, bring back to the boil and cook for 10–12 minutes, until tender but still firm to the bite. Drain and set aside.

2 Cut the broccoli into florets and cook in salted boiling water for 5 minutes. Drain, rinse with cold water and drain again.

3 Heat the olive oil in the pan that the pasta was cooked in. Add the garlic, chillies and tomatoes, if using. Cook over a high heat for 1 minute.

4 Add the broccoli to the pan and mix well. Cook for 2 minutes to heat through. Add the pasta and mix well again. Cook for 1 minute longer.

5 Remove the pasta from the heat, turn into a large serving bowl and serve garnished with basil.

creamy ricotta, mint & garlic pasta

SERVES 4

300 g/10½ oz short fresh pasta shapes

140 g/5 oz ricotta cheese

1–2 roasted garlic cloves from a jar, finely chopped

150 ml/5 fl oz double cream

1 tbsp chopped fresh mint and 4 sprigs, to garnish

salt and pepper

1 Bring a large saucepan of lightly salted water to the boil. Add the pasta, bring back to the boil and cook for 4–6 minutes, until tender but still firm to the bite.

2 Beat the ricotta, garlic, cream and chopped mint together in a bowl until smooth.

3 Drain the cooked pasta then tip back into the pan. Pour in the cheese mixture and toss together.

4 Season with pepper and serve immediately, garnished with the sprigs of mint.

spaghetti with parsley & parmesan

SERVES 4

450 g/1 lb dried spaghetti

175 g/6 oz unsalted butter

4 tbsp chopped fresh flat-leaf parsley

225 g/8 oz Parmesan-style vegetarian cheese, grated

salt

1 Bring a large saucepan of lightly salted water to the boil. Add the pasta, bring back to the boil and cook for 10–12 minutes, until tender but still firm to the bite. Drain and tip into a warmed serving dish.

2 Add the butter, parsley and half the Parmesan-style vegetarian cheese and toss well, using 2 forks, until the butter and cheese have melted. Serve immediately with the remaining Parmesan-style vegetarian cheese handed separately.

VARIATION

For a bit of colour, add a handful of cherry tomatoes to the dish. Cut them in half and add them to the pasta with the butter and parsley.

4

Sensational Sides

potatoes dauphinois

SERVES 4

1 tbsp butter, for greasing

675 g/1½ lb waxy potatoes, sliced

2 garlic cloves, crushed

1 red onion, sliced

85 g/3 oz Gruyère cheese, grated

300 ml/½ pint double cream

salt and pepper

1 Preheat the oven to 180°C/350°F/Gas Mark 4. Lightly grease a 1-litre/1¾-pint shallow ovenproof dish with butter.

2 Arrange a single layer of potato slices in the base of the prepared dish.

3 Top the potato slices with half the garlic, half the sliced red onion and one third of the grated Gruyère cheese. Season to taste with a little salt and some pepper.

4 Repeat the layers in exactly the same order, finishing with a layer of potatoes topped with grated cheese.

5 Pour the cream over the top of the potatoes and bake in the oven for 1½ hours, or until the potatoes are cooked through and the top is browned and crispy. Serve the potatoes at once, straight from the dish.

herby potatoes & onion

SERVES 4

900 g/2 lb waxy potatoes, cut into cubes

125 g/4½ oz butter

1 red onion, cut into 8 wedges

2 garlic cloves, crushed

1 tsp lemon juice

2 tbsp chopped fresh thyme

salt and pepper

1 Cook the cubed potatoes in a saucepan of boiling salted water for 10 minutes. Drain thoroughly.

2 Melt the butter in a large, heavy-based frying pan and add the red onion wedges, garlic and lemon juice. Cook, stirring constantly for 2–3 minutes.

3 Add the potatoes to the pan and mix well to coat in the butter mixture.

4 Reduce the heat, cover and cook for 25–30 minutes, or until the potatoes are golden brown and tender.

5 Sprinkle the chopped thyme over the top of the potatoes and season to taste with salt and pepper. Transfer to a warm serving dish and serve immediately.

garlic mash

SERVES 4

900 g/2 lb floury potatoes, cut into chunks

8 garlic cloves, crushed

150 ml/5 fl oz milk

85 g/3 oz butter, plus extra to garnish

pinch of freshly grated nutmeg

salt and pepper

1 tbsp chopped fresh flat-leaf parsley, to garnish

1 Put the potatoes in a large saucepan. Add enough cold water to cover and a pinch of salt. Bring to the boil and cook for 10 minutes. Add the garlic and cook for 10 minutes more, until the potatoes are tender.

2 Drain the potatoes and garlic thoroughly, reserving 3 tablespoons of the cooking liquid.

3 Return the reserved liquid to the pan, add the milk and bring to simmering point. Add the butter and return the potatoes and garlic to the pan. Mash thoroughly with a potato masher.

4 Season to taste with nutmeg and salt and pepper and beat the potato mixture with a wooden spoon until light and fluffy. Garnish with flat-leaf parsley and a large knob of butter and serve immediately.

bombay potatoes

SERVES 4

1 kg/2 lb 4 oz waxy potatoes

2 tbsp vegetable ghee

1 tsp panch poran spice mix

3 tsp ground turmeric

2 tbsp tomato purée

300 ml/10 fl oz plain yogurt

salt

chopped fresh coriander, to garnish

1 Preheat the oven to 180°C/350°F/Gas Mark 4. Put the whole potatoes into a large saucepan of salted cold water. Bring to the boil, then simmer for about 15 minutes, until the potatoes are just cooked, but not tender.

2 Heat the ghee in a separate saucepan over medium heat and add the panch poran, turmeric, tomato purée, yogurt and salt. Bring to the boil and simmer, uncovered, for 5 minutes.

3 Drain the potatoes and cut each one into 4 pieces. Add the potatoes to the pan, then cover and cook briefly. Transfer to an ovenproof casserole. Cook in the oven for about 40 minutes, or until the potatoes are tender and the sauce has thickened a little. Sprinkle with chopped coriander and serve immediately.

pesto potatoes

SERVES 4

900 g/2 lb small new potatoes

75 g/2¾ oz fresh basil

2 tbsp pine kernels

3 garlic cloves, crushed

100 ml/3½ fl oz olive oil

75 g/2¾ oz mixed Parmesan-style vegetarian and pecorino cheeses, grated

salt and pepper

fresh basil sprigs, to garnish

1 Cook the potatoes in a saucepan of boiling salted water for 15 minutes or until tender. Drain well, transfer to a warmed serving dish and keep warm until required.

2 Meanwhile, put the fresh basil, pine kernels, crushed garlic and a little salt and pepper to taste in a food processor. Blend for 30 seconds, adding the oil gradually, until smooth.

3 Remove the mixture from the food processor and transfer it to a mixing bowl. Stir in the grated Parmesan-style vegetarian and pecorino cheeses.

4 Spoon the pesto sauce over the potatoes and mix well. Garnish with fresh basil sprigs and serve immediately.

colcannon

SERVES 4

225 g/8 oz green cabbage, shredded

5 tbsp milk

225 g/8 oz floury potatoes, diced

1 large leek, chopped

pinch of freshly grated nutmeg

knob of butter

salt and pepper

1 Cook the shredded cabbage in a saucepan of boiling salted water for 7–10 minutes. Drain thoroughly and set aside.

2 Meanwhile, in a separate saucepan, bring the milk to the boil and add the potatoes and leek. Reduce the heat and simmer for 15–20 minutes, or until they are cooked through.

3 Remove from the heat, stir in the freshly grated nutmeg and thoroughly mash the potatoes and leek together.

4 Add the drained cabbage to the mashed potato and leek mixture, season to taste and mix together well.

5 Spoon the mixture into a warmed serving dish, making a hollow in the centre with the back of a spoon.

6 Place the butter on top and serve the colcannon at once, while it is still hot.

chargrilled vegetables

SERVES 6

2 sweet potatoes, sliced

3 courgettes, halved lengthways

3 red peppers, deseeded and cut into quarters

olive oil, for brushing

salt

salsa verde

2 fresh green chillies, halved and deseeded

8 spring onions, roughly chopped

2 garlic cloves, roughly chopped

1 tbsp capers

bunch of fresh parsley, roughly chopped

grated rind and juice of 1 lime

4 tbsp lemon juice

6 tbsp olive oil

1 tbsp green Tabasco sauce

pepper

1 Preheat the grill. Cook the sweet potato slices in boiling water for 5 minutes. Drain and set aside to cool. Sprinkle the courgettes with salt and set aside for 30 minutes. Rinse and pat dry with kitchen paper.

2 Meanwhile, make the salsa verde. Put the chillies, spring onions and garlic in a food processor and process briefly. Add the capers and parsley and pulse until finely chopped. Transfer the mixture to a serving bowl.

3 Stir in the lime rind and juice, lemon juice, olive oil and Tabasco. Season to taste with pepper, cover with clingfilm and chill in the refrigerator until required.

4 Brush the sweet potato slices, courgettes and peppers with olive oil and spread out on a grill rack or barbecue. Grill, turning once and brushing with more olive oil, for 8–10 minutes, until tender and lightly charred. Serve the vegetables immediately with the salsa verde.

couscous salad with roasted butternut squash

SERVES 4

2 tbsp honey

4 tbsp olive oil

1 butternut squash, peeled, deseeded and cut into 2-cm/¾-inch chunks

250 g/9 oz couscous

400 ml/14 fl oz low-salt vegetable stock

½ cucumber, diced

1 courgette, diced

1 red pepper, deseeded and diced

juice of ½ lemon

2 tbsp chopped fresh parsley

salt and pepper

1 Preheat the oven to 190°C/375°F/Gas Mark 5. Mix half the honey with 1 tablespoon of the oil in a large bowl, add the squash and toss well to coat. Tip into a roasting tin and roast in the preheated oven for 30–40 minutes until soft and golden.

2 Meanwhile, put the couscous in a heatproof bowl. Heat the stock in a saucepan and pour over the couscous, cover and leave for 3 minutes. Add 1 tablespoon of the remaining oil and fork through, then stir in the diced cucumber, courgette and red pepper. Re-cover and keep warm.

3 Whisk the remaining honey and oil with the lemon juice in a jug and season to taste with salt and pepper. Stir the mixture through the couscous.

4 To serve, top the couscous with the roasted squash and sprinkle with the parsley.

steamed vegetable parcels

SERVES 4

115 g/4 oz **French beans**

55 g/2 oz **mangetouts**

12 **baby carrots**

8 **baby onions or shallots**

12 **baby turnips**

8 **radishes**

55 g/2 oz **unsalted butter or margarine**

4 **thinly pared strips of lemon rind**

4 tsp **finely chopped fresh chervil**

4 tbsp **dry white wine**

salt and pepper

1 Cut out 4 double thickness rounds of greaseproof paper about 30 cm/12 inches in diameter.

2 Divide the French beans, mangetouts, carrots, onions, turnips and radishes among the rounds, placing them on one half. Season to taste with salt and pepper and dot with the butter. Add a strip of lemon rind to each. Sprinkle with the chervil and drizzle with the wine. Fold over the double layer of paper, twisting the edges together to seal.

3 Bring a large pan of water to the boil and place a steamer on top. Put the parcels in the steamer, cover tightly and steam for 8–10 minutes. Serve the parcels immediately, to be unwrapped at the table.

roasted vegetables

SERVES 4

1 onion, cut into wedges

2–4 garlic cloves, left whole but peeled

1 aubergine, about 225 g/ 8 oz, trimmed and cut into cubes

2 courgettes, about 175 g/ 6 oz, trimmed and cut into chunks

300 g/10½ oz butternut squash, peeled, deseeded and cut into small wedges

2 assorted coloured peppers, deseeded and cut into chunks

2 tsp olive oil

1 tbsp shredded fresh basil

pepper

1 Preheat the oven to 200°C/400°F/Gas Mark 6. Place the onion wedges, whole garlic cloves and aubergine cubes in a large roasting tin.

2 Add the courgettes, squash and peppers to the roasting tin then pour over the oil. Turn the vegetables until they are lightly coated in the oil.

3 Roast the vegetables for 35–40 minutes, or until softened but not mushy. Turn the vegetables over occasionally during cooking.

4 Remove the vegetables from the oven, season with pepper to taste and stir. Scatter with shredded basil and serve, divided between 4 warmed bowls, while still warm.

chinese vegetables

SERVES 4

2 tbsp groundnut oil

350 g/12 oz broccoli florets

1 tbsp chopped fresh ginger

2 onions, cut into 8 pieces

3 celery sticks, sliced

175 g/6 oz baby spinach

125 g/4½ oz mangetouts

6 spring onions, quartered

2 garlic cloves, crushed

2 tbsp light soy sauce

2 tsp caster sugar

2 tbsp dry sherry

1 tbsp hoisin sauce

150 ml/5 fl oz vegetable stock

1 Heat the groundnut oil in a preheated wok until it is almost smoking. Add the broccoli florets, chopped ginger, onions and celery to the wok and stir-fry for 1 minute.

2 Add the spinach, mangetouts, spring onions and garlic and stir-fry for 3–4 minutes. Mix together the soy sauce, caster sugar, sherry, hoisin sauce and vegetable stock.

3 Pour the stock mixture into the wok, mixing well to coat the vegetables. Cover the wok and cook over a medium heat for 2–3 minutes, or until the vegetables are cooked through, but still crisp.

4 Transfer the Chinese vegetables to a warmed serving dish and serve immediately.

spicy pak choi with sesame sauce

SERVES 4

2 tsp groundnut or vegetable oil

1 red chilli, deseeded and thinly sliced

1 garlic clove, thinly sliced

5 small pak choi, quartered

100ml / 3½ fl oz vegetable stock

sauce

25 g/1 oz sesame seeds

2 tbsp dark soy sauce

2 tsp soft light brown sugar

1 garlic clove, crushed

3 tbsp sesame oil

1 For the sesame sauce, toast the sesame seeds in a dry frying pan set over a medium heat, stirring until lightly browned. Remove from the heat and cool slightly. Transfer to a pestle and mortar. Add the soy sauce, sugar and crushed garlic and pound to a coarse paste. Stir in the sesame oil.

2 Heat the groundnut oil in a wok or large frying pan. Add the chilli and sliced garlic and stir-fry for 20–30 seconds. Add the pak choi and stir-fry for 5 minutes, adding the stock a little at a time to prevent sticking.

3 Transfer the pak choi to a warmed dish, drizzle the sesame sauce over the top and serve immediately.

chinese-style gingered vegetables

SERVES 2

1 tbsp sunflower or groundnut oil

2.5-cm/1-inch piece fresh ginger, peeled and grated

1 onion, thinly sliced

115 g/4 oz frozen French beans, cut into small pieces

450 g/1 lb bag frozen mixed vegetables

150 ml/5 fl oz water

2 heaped tbsp dark brown sugar

2 tbsp cornflour

4 tbsp malt vinegar

4 tbsp soy sauce

1 tsp ground ginger

1 Heat the oil in a wok or large frying pan, add the grated ginger and fry for 1 minute. Remove from the wok or pan and drain on kitchen paper.

2 Reduce the heat slightly and add the vegetables and water to the wok.

3 Cover with a lid or foil and cook for 5–6 minutes, or until the vegetables are tender.

4 Mix the sugar, cornflour, malt vinegar, soy sauce and ground ginger together in a bowl. Increase the heat to medium and add the mixture to the vegetables in the wok. Simmer for 1 minute, stirring, until thickened.

5 Return the ginger to the wok and stir to mix well. Heat through for 2 minutes and then serve immediately.

mixed cabbage coleslaw

SERVES 4

85 g/3 oz red cabbage

85 g/3 oz hard white cabbage

55 g/2 oz green cabbage

2 carrots, about 175 g/6 oz, peeled and grated

1 white onion, finely sliced

2 red apples, cored and chopped

4 tbsp orange juice

2 celery sticks, trimmed and finely sliced

55 g/2 oz canned sweetcorn kernels

2 tbsp raisins

dressing

4 tbsp low fat natural yogurt

1 tbsp chopped fresh parsley

pepper

1 Discard the outer leaves and hard central core from the cabbages and shred finely. Wash well in plenty of cold water and drain thoroughly.

2 Place the cabbages in a bowl and stir in the carrots and onion. Toss the apples in the orange juice and add to the cabbages together with any remaining orange juice, and the celery, sweetcorn and raisins. Mix well.

3 For the dressing, mix the yogurt, parsley and pepper to taste in a bowl, then pour over the cabbage mixture. Stir and serve.

spiced lentils with spinach

SERVES 4–6

2 tbsp olive oil

1 large onion, finely chopped

1 large garlic clove, crushed

½ tbsp ground cumin

½ tsp ground ginger

250 g/9 oz Puy lentils

about 600 ml/1 pint vegetable stock

100 g/3½ oz baby spinach leaves

2 tbsp fresh mint leaves

1 tbsp fresh coriander leaves

1 tbsp fresh flat-leaf parsley

lemon juice

salt and pepper

strips of lemon rind, to garnish

1 Heat the oil in a large frying pan over a medium heat. Add the onion and cook, stirring occasionally, for about 6 minutes. Stir in the garlic, cumin and ginger and cook, stirring occasionally, until the onion starts to brown.

2 Stir in the lentils. Pour in enough stock to cover the lentils by 2.5 cm/1 inch and bring to the boil. Lower the heat and simmer for 20–30 minutes until the lentils are tender.

3 Meanwhile, rinse the spinach leaves in several changes of cold water and shake dry. Finely chop the mint, coriander leaves and parsley.

4 If there isn't any stock left in the pan, add a little extra. Add the spinach and stir through until it just wilts. Stir in the mint, coriander and parsley. Adjust the seasoning, adding lemon juice and salt and pepper. Transfer to a serving bowl and serve, garnished with lemon rind.

mexican rice

SERVES 4

1 onion, chopped

400 g/14 oz plum tomatoes, peeled, deseeded and chopped

250 ml/9 fl oz vegetable stock

200 g/7 oz long-grain rice

salt and pepper

1 Put the onion and tomatoes in a food processor and process to a smooth purée. Scrape the purée into a saucepan, pour in the stock and bring to the boil over a medium heat, stirring occasionally.

2 Add the rice and stir once, then reduce the heat, cover and simmer for 20–25 minutes until all the liquid has been absorbed and the rice is tender. Season to taste with salt and pepper and serve immediately.

crispy roast asparagus

SERVES 4

450 g/1 lb asparagus spears

2 tbsp extra virgin olive oil

1 tsp coarse sea salt

1 tbsp grated Parmesan-style vegetarian cheese, to serve

1 Preheat the oven to 200°C/400°F/Gas Mark 6. Choose asparagus spears of similar widths. Trim the base of the spears so that all the stems are approximately the same length.

2 Arrange the asparagus in a single layer on a metal baking sheet. Drizzle with olive oil and sprinkle with salt.

3 Place the tray in the oven and bake for 10–15 minutes, turning once. Remove from the oven, transfer to a warmed serving dish and serve immediately, sprinkled with the grated Parmesan-style vegetarian cheese.

hot roast peppers

SERVES 6

6 red peppers, deseeded and cut into thick strips

140 g/5 oz fresh green serrano or jalapeño chillies, deseeded and sliced into thin strips

2 garlic cloves, crushed

4 tbsp extra virgin olive oil

1 Preheat the oven to 200°C/400°F/Gas Mark 6. Put the peppers, chillies and garlic in a shallow casserole dish. Pour in the oil.

2 Cover and bake for 50–60 minutes, or until the peppers have softened. Remove the lid and reduce the temperature to 180°C/350°F/Gas Mark 4. Return the casserole dish to the oven and bake for a further 45 minutes, or until the peppers are very soft and beginning to char.

3 Serve immediately if serving hot. Alternatively, leave to cool, then transfer to a large screw-top jar and store in the refrigerator for up to 3 weeks, topped up with more olive oil to keep the peppers covered, if necessary.

lemon &
garlic spinach

SERVES 4

4 tbsp olive oil

**2 garlic cloves, thinly
sliced**

**450 g/1 lb fresh spinach,
torn or shredded**

juice of ½ lemon

salt and pepper

1 Heat the olive oil on a high heat in a large frying pan.
Add the garlic and spinach and cook, stirring constantly,
until the spinach is soft. Take care not to let the spinach burn.

2 Remove from the heat, turn into a serving bowl and
sprinkle with lemon juice. Season with salt and pepper.
Mix well and serve either hot or at room temperature.

stir-fried broccoli

SERVES 4

2 tbsp vegetable oil

2 broccoli heads, cut into florets

2 tbsp soy sauce

1 tsp cornflour

1 tbsp caster sugar

1 tsp grated fresh ginger

1 garlic clove, crushed

pinch of dried red pepper flakes

1 tsp toasted sesame seeds, to garnish

1 Heat the oil in a large preheated wok or skillet over high heat until almost smoking. Add the broccoli and stir-fry for 4–5 minutes. Reduce the heat to medium.

2 Combine the soy sauce, cornflour, sugar, ginger, garlic and red pepper flakes in a small bowl. Add the mixture to the broccoli and cook, stirring constantly, for 2–3 minutes until the sauce thickens slightly.

3 Transfer to a warmed serving dish, garnish with the sesame seeds and serve immediately.

lemon beans

SERVES 4

**900 g/2 lb mixed green
beans, such as broad
beans, French beans,
runner beans**

**75 g/2½ oz butter or
margarine**

4 tsp plain flour

**300 ml/½ pint vegetable
stock**

5 tbsp dry white wine

6 tbsp single cream

**3 tbsp chopped fresh mixed
herbs**

grated rind of 1 lemon

2 tbsp lemon juice

salt and pepper

1 Cook the beans in a saucepan of boiling salted water for 10 minutes, or until tender. Drain and place in a warmed serving dish.

2 Meanwhile, melt the butter in a saucepan. Add the flour and cook, stirring constantly, for 1 minute. Remove the pan from the heat and gradually stir in the stock and wine. Return the pan to the heat and bring to the boil, stirring.

3 Remove the pan from the heat once again and stir in the single cream, mixed herbs, lemon rind and juice. Season to taste with salt and pepper. Pour the sauce over the beans, mixing well to coat thoroughly. Serve immediately.

peas with baby onions

SERVES 4

15 g/½ oz unsalted butter

175 g/6 oz baby onions

900 g/2 lb fresh peas, shelled

125 ml/4 fl oz water

2 tbsp plain flour

150 ml/5 fl oz double cream

1 tbsp chopped fresh parsley

1 tbsp lemon juice

salt and pepper

1 Melt the butter in a large, heavy-based saucepan. Add the whole baby onions and cook, stirring occasionally, for 5 minutes. Add the peas and cook, stirring constantly, for a further 3 minutes, then add the measured water and bring to the boil. Lower the heat, partially cover and simmer for 10 minutes.

2 Beat the flour into the cream. Remove the pan from the heat and stir in the cream mixture and parsley and season to taste with salt and pepper.

3 Return the pan to the heat and cook, stirring gently but constantly, for about 3 minutes, until thickened.

4 Stir the lemon juice into the sauce and serve the peas immediately.

red cabbage &
beetroot slaw

SERVES 4

**350 g/12 oz red cabbage,
finely shredded**

**175 g/6 oz cooked
beetroot, sliced into thin
matchsticks**

**1 apple, cored and thinly
sliced**

1 tbsp lemon juice

1 tbsp sunflower seeds

1 tbsp pumpkin seeds

salt and pepper

dressing

3 tbsp mayonnaise

2 tbsp Greek yogurt

1 tbsp red wine vinegar

1 Place the cabbage, beetroot and apple slices in a large bowl. Add the lemon juice and mix well.

2 To make the dressing, place the mayonnaise, yogurt and red wine vinegar in a bowl and mix together until smooth. Pour over the salad and stir well. Season with salt and pepper and cover and chill in the refrigerator for at least 1 hour.

3 Stir the salad thoroughly and adjust the seasoning to taste. Sprinkle with the sunflower and pumpkin seeds just before serving.

spiced basmati rice

SERVES 4

225 g/8 oz basmati rice

25 g/1 oz ghee or 2 tbsp vegetable oil or groundnut oil

5 green cardamom pods, bruised

5 cloves

½ cinnamon stick

1 tsp fennel seeds

½ tsp black mustard seeds

2 bay leaves

450 ml/16 fl oz water

1½ tsp salt, or to taste

2 tbsp chopped fresh coriander

pepper

1 Rinse the rice in several changes of water until the water runs clear, then leave to soak for 30 minutes. Drain and set aside until ready to cook.

2 Heat a casserole or large saucepan with a tight-fitting lid over a medium–high heat, then add the ghee. Add the spices and bay leaves and stir for 30 seconds. Stir the rice into the casserole so the grains are coated with ghee. Stir in the water and salt and bring to the boil.

3 Reduce the heat to as low as possible and cover the casserole tightly. Simmer, without lifting the lid, for 8–10 minutes, until the grains are tender and all the liquid has been absorbed.

4 Turn off the heat and use two forks to mix in the coriander. Adjust the seasoning to taste. Re-cover the pan and leave to stand for 5 minutes before serving.

VARIATION

For a bit of colour and texture, finely chop some French beans or mangetout and fry for a few minutes. Stir through the rice and serve.